Romy Rüegger

AF328491

Scripts
for Performances

Language is Skin

Archive Books

Note

What happened, with whom and where:

Who ever said a performance has anything to do with the refusal of speech, expressive gesturing, acting skills and nakedness?
THIS IS WRONG!

Go to the theater if you want to see a theater performance. For someone who likes to share one's sweat and nakedness – the sauna at the lake is great.

Imagine a space that is built by shifting the margins and the centres of collective memories. Overlapping and layering, times and spaces. All here, all present, listening. Sound joined rooms, imaginary friends and shared futures. Writing and change. Divas, paragons, stone butches, fortune tellers, witches. Scammers and shape shifters. Idealized figures and background listeners. Crossing and alternating sequences – projected, described, transmitted.

Several subcutaneous organs produce our speech, allowing words to find their way from one body to another. A happy epitome? A language that listens as it speaks. Imagination, sisterhood, difference. Now, more now than ever: now.

A constellation of texts, images and movements, mostly written to be spoken, projected and performed, made accessible for silent reading. The scripts as they are printed do not document the performances primarily. They are indications of spatial and temporal layerings and juxtapositions of aesthetic and poetic elements and bodies.

Overlapping everyday observations with archival material – confronting, jumping. Figures that intervene. Interruptions in the reproduction and maintenance of colonial poison cabinets, of *white* and patriarchal canons. Taking care of. Trouble, always trouble.

In most texts no fixed positions are indicated for the spectators or listeners. They were invited to step inside the performative space. Stepping in and taking a seat, as one does in reading them now, silently. The imagination might turn in the other direction. Towards the tones of the voices speaking those texts, the recordings, life. Close readings of

social power relationships and the value systems and technologies at work in searching, describing and imagining histories as involvements and possibilities for structural change.

The sequences of movements and montages performed are friable, fragile. Sight axes often contradict with what one can hear. Engaging listening as a main capacity. The actions performed are subtle – dismantling, confronting, undoing, suggesting articulations to come. Sometimes they slip, between the lines, as the bodies turn, get lost or seduced, in each other's gaze.

Thank you for sharing and imagining. Multiple toned voices, silent sequences, mediocre aesthetics, weak art and crimes against genre. What are the background noises and music, the social spaces and subject positions, along and through which you read these texts?
Let me know!

Markups for voices, movements and sounds:

What is spoken live by reading from a paper, a book, a projection, a foil or after headphones is set in plain text. *Recorded voices, sound footage or lyrics are set in italics.* [Movements, actions and additional descriptions of what can be heard or seen are mentioned in brackets].
The performances were often site specific and sometimes adjusted for being re-performed in other spaces or translated into a video, an exhibition contribution, for being printed or broadcasted. The subtitle of each work specify the version of the scripts included into this publication.

A turbine production plant on the one side of the river. On the other, a housing cooperative for working women. The former industrial sites are under reconstruction now: the invention of a history as it never was. The action is the every day, in continued present tenses. The performance takes place at the former Escher Wyss Material Testing Institute in Zurich.

It is a montage of repeating images on two projectors. Modulated consecutive translation notes from current administrative processes in migration offices and images from the archives of the housing cooperative and the city, the performer' and the spectators' bodies moving in and out of it.

Markings on the floor superimpose a floor plan of a woman's apartment on the given production space. Recorded voices come from different directions, some from behind the wall of a built-in cube, that separates the exhibitions space from the gallery's storage.

Sound of tearing
down former
Escher Wyss
factory buildings

Si tu vivais ici tu serais déjà chez toi.

A sketch that remains a sketch – as the title already
says: you might, you would.

It happens in private, even if the questions that
are discussed, are public ones. A private space that
is a public one, without becoming public. Talking
privately, integrating privately, administrating
intimacy.

– It is nothing small that is being negotiated here

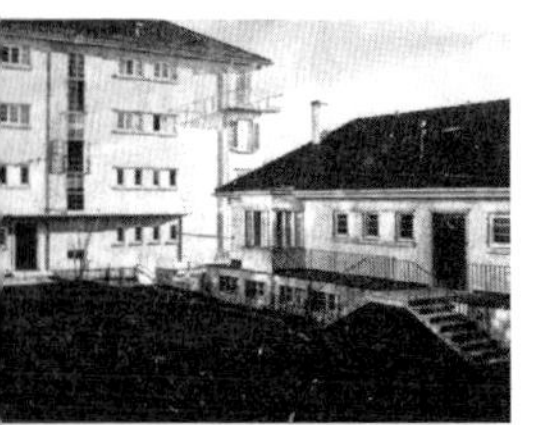

[Projetion on the front wall of the built-in cube]

You enter the room through the front door. Nobody stops you. Here, nobody stops you. Through the entrance door, which earlier was already a door, slips a white-washed character. What has she already done today? Should something have happened to her?

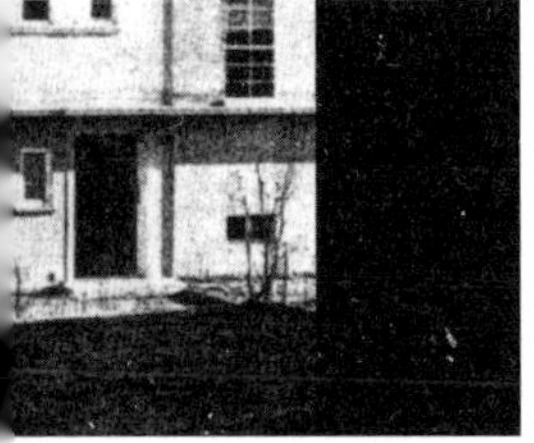

[Walking towards the entrance door of the exhibition space]

– *Rarely something happens.*

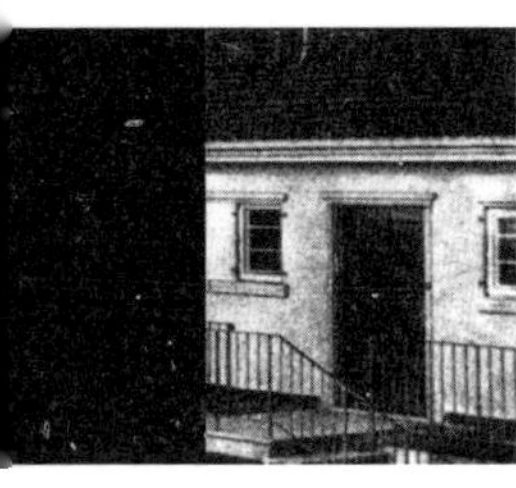

La defensa could be everywhere, but it's not.

Taking notes of a conversation. With the methods of translators, simultaneously. Constellations of signs that follow protocols to record exactly what was said, even if linearity and clarity are lost in the conversation.

It is a long conversation. What is said should remain in secrecy. What remains are the notes of the translator, a testimony of the bodies through which what was said has streamed, from one language into another one. Also the notes are secret.

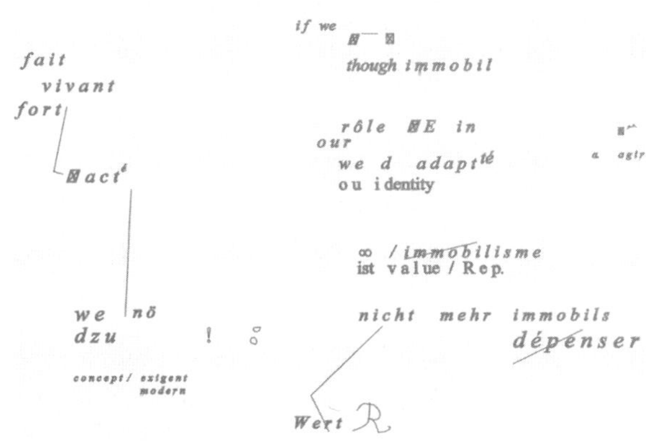

In the back of the room appears a second projection with notes

The entire administrative procedure of social code conversion happens secretly. Th e translators that accompany these processes, through which the fugitive are getting inscribed as refugees, are bound to offi cial discretion. It is said that the notes are the way they are, because there is little time.

If we / Do this or that / We are though immobile / Our role in / We do adapt / Our identity / We have been adapted / To our identity / Endless is not / immobilism / Endless is the production of value – let's break repetition / If we are no longer immobile / We are spending our / We are spending our identity for money for taxes / If we are no longer immobile / We are spending our knowledge / For values to change / A for Agir: Act / How do we / Faire vivre fort and act / How do we / Make a strong living, to act / For no / We put a no to that / Concepts have been calling / Calling is modern / Concepts have been calling. For modern values to be changed.

[Getting dressed with several masks]

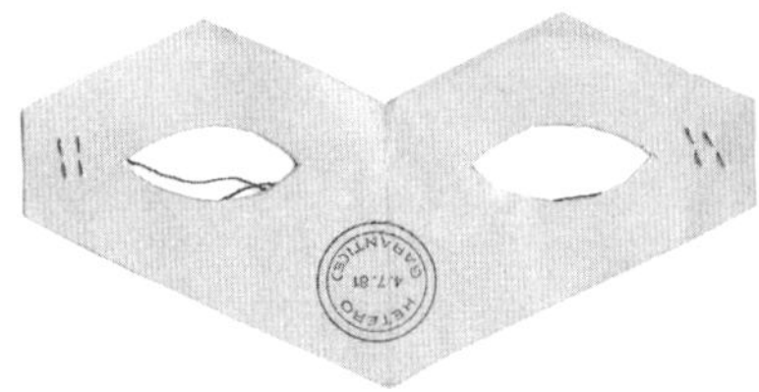

[Opening the window towards the main hall of the former
Escher Wyss factory site, climbing up to sit on the window
frame. Sound of demolition works in the background.
Reading from a little book]

'We speak languages that are not ours, we walk
around without passports or identity papers.'

It is seven o'clock. The train from Zurich to Milan
crosses the border in Chiasso. It stops. A stop that
is not noted in the train's schedule. It is getting
quiet. What is going on? What is this all about?
Nothing linear, as you can see. No stringent narrative
or storyline, no clear sequence or procedure. The
histories of the administration, management and
maintenance of bodies and their domestication,
nameless mostly – It's going to be complicated.

[Placing additional tapes on the floor to mark the floor
plan of one of the women's one room appartements]

*Sleeping in a name, eating in an other, loving with
a third, working without.*

[Standing on the line where the red brick floor of the former
reception meets the concrete floor where the machines were
placed]

Here she works: a red brick floor. Behind the room divider: the Material Testing Institute of Escher Wyss. She works at the reception.

[Glimpse of a worker and palets of blank grenades]

The world needs: iron, steel, metals. Ship's turbines, turbo turbines, steam turbines.

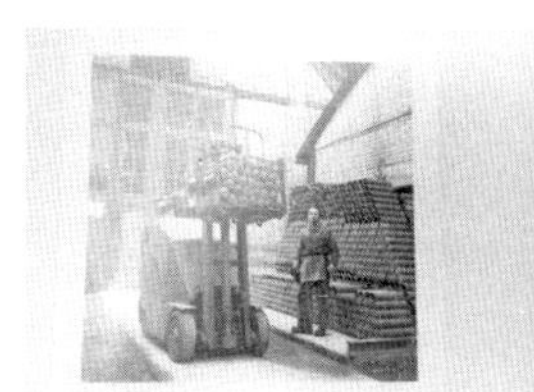

She says: nobody needs this.

It is 1926, the years between the wars. The female body is once more being constructed as both adjective and workforce. A non-domestic domestication, this time in the name of progress and control.

[Stepping into the projection. Taking an empty equipment box, a kitchen radio and an audio player along]

Here she hangs up her clothes after work, when she arrives at home

[Steps]

Here she sits and looks outside

[Steps]

Here she sleeps

[Steps]

There is a round carpet on the floor, especially in winter

[Steps]

Here she washes her hands, her face

[Steps]

The bath room is outside, shared with the other women of the same floor

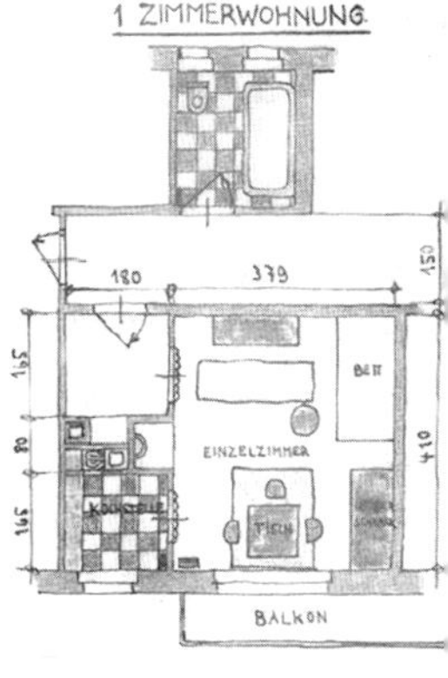

Here is the entrance of the appartement, here she enters, here she leaves

[Steps]

Here public voices enter her private space: This is her radio

[Steps]

[Placing the radio in the 'kitchen']

'Hellow. Today we do what we can. And thank you for being here.'

Living alone for women around 1926 is almost impossible. The Housing Cooperative of Working Women begins to build. A social project in the 'Red Zurich' of the interwar period with its labor movements and foundations of cooperatives. 500 meters north of here, of the Material Testing Institute of Escher Wyss, on the other side of the river. Women are needed in the industrial workforce. The idea of small appartements, that are easy to maintain, for single women working outside of the home, is therefore supported, and their building financed by the city.

Projection off   *I entered the room in the same way, as one happens to enter a dream.*

[Taking a seat on the empty equipment box]

Behind me the city. The scenery of it. No, I am not from here. Only the language that I carry is ment to be. To be at home in a language, in other people's stories. Living in the stories of others.

A you, a she, a we.

She is in exile, she says, and is about to tell you a
story, a story that suits the scenery, a story from here.

*'We speak languages that are not ours, we walk
around without passports or identity papers.'*

[Stepping out of what is marked as private space, taking the
empty equipment box along]

Again: the train stops in Chiasso, just like that. The
carriage is almost empty. The usual border police
walk through the train compartments. Their gaze
wanders with scrutiny, glances.

[Sitting down on the empty equipment box, below the
window]

If you lived here you would already be at yours.

In the back of the
room re-appears a
second projection

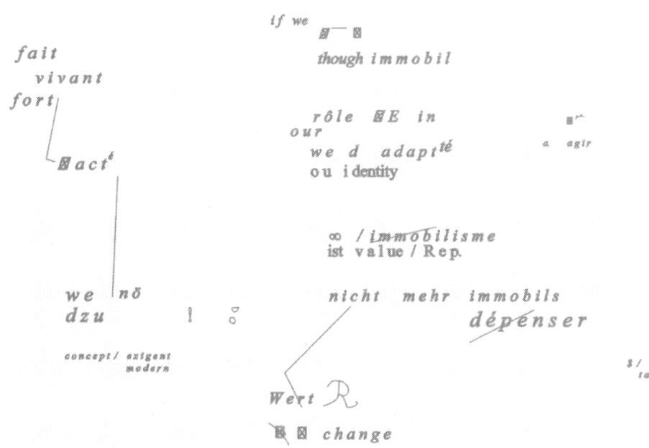

This is the summary of a conversation. The way
I remember it. In secrecy. The summary is meant
to remind the memory, to persuade it to be what
it is: a turnaround, a reassembly of what might
have happened. What was said. Maybe like that,
in this sequence, with these gaps, with these
foreshadowing hints. Of course not like that,
because everything happens behind closed doors,
in privacy. Like that, alike. Alike in comparision
to memory.

What opens up between two fields of language.
A place in between. Between the inbetweens.
Walking around in the inbetweens.

[Stepping back into the projection. Sitting down on the
empty equipment box, beside where the kitchen radio has
been left before]

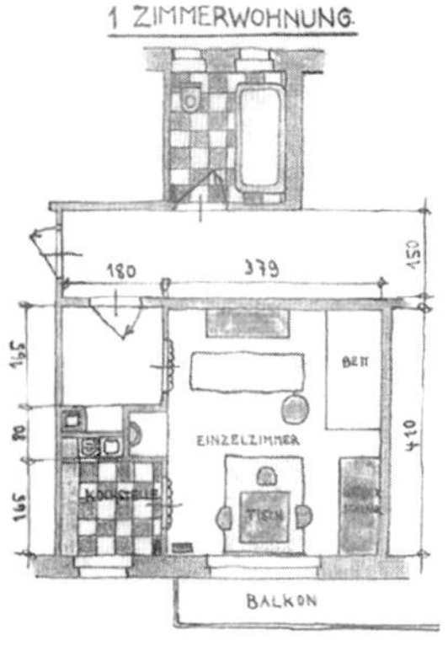

'Domestic space was, in the interwar period, emotion-
ally and symbolically constructed as a feminine sphere
– a place of the mundane, belonging to women. How
radios were placed within the living room. The place-
ment and control of the radio and later television in
the home needs to be seen as part of the contestation
that takes place over the meaning and practices of
domesticity and private lives. The private world of
the domestic space relies upon an ostensible otherness
of the public world. In this version, the apparently
timeless feminine values of intimacy and authenticity
are set against the masculine experience of alienation
and dehumanisation that constitute modern history.
The wireless, a symbol of modernity, crossed the
boundaries between public and private, masculine
and feminine spheres.'

[From behind the same wall on which the image is projected
a record plays]

*'My first letter is double-u. I've never been known.
I'm not in your history, your heart or your soul. Your
paintings and pictures don't show my real face. You
cut me and wrap me in ribbons and lace.'*

A name is like a room. Others have lived in it before,
leaving their traces. Once I wanted to drill a hole
into one of the walls. Everywhere that I drilled,
there was already a hole under the paint.

Dressing with a name, the way one dresses with a
jacket. Sharing a name, the way one shares clothes
with sisters. Filling a name, the way one fills a
t-shirt, which was filled before by a sister, a friend.
A bit too much space for the shoulders, a bit too
little for the hips.

[Addressing the person in the public that chose to stand
where the bed would be]

Excuse me, you are standing on my bed.

This is the size of my room, of my apartment
even. It seems to be a given, that this room, this
apartment exists, in this size. But it's not. People
have been fighting for it.

The Industry booms. Zurich is red. Houses are built
cooperatively. For families, family apartment. But
not everyone wants to live like this. It wasn't only
new ways of working that came with the growth of
industry, but also new forms of living.

How important a private space is, and what that private space is, to be a person. Zurich 1926 and today.

Stories are material, they are being produced by someone, re-narrated, circulated, traded. They act. They act in the everyday. War can be an everyday. Testing war material, testing the materiality of war can be an everyday.

And women in this war, what do they do in this war.

She stands at the reception, in the archive of materials of the Material Testing Institute of Escher Wyss. You want to know, how I am telling you my story, in which language and under which name?

I walked to work across that little bridge for pedestrians. Not over the viaduct – a train runs over the viaduct, still right now, every now and then. I would like you to see that everything is connected – the turbines that are produced here, the raw materials, the exploitation of these materials, the inner and the outer colonisation, modern forms of living, welfare, modernity, the modern welfare state, and we.

'My first letter is double-u. I've never been known. I'm not in your history, your heart or your soul. Your paintings and pictures don't show my real face. You cut me and wrap me in ribbons and lace.'

[Stepping into the projection]

Excuse me. You are standing on my bed.

[Taking off jacket]

Here is where Lux Guyer, architect of the Housing Cooperative for Working Women in 1925, planned that I sleep

[Steps]

Here, that I sit by the window and read. Read by daylight

[Steps]

Here, that I wash my hands and my face

[Steps]

[Turning around]

Excuse me, you are standing in my view. The view of the river and the industrial district. Every hour a train stops down here at Letten station.

Woman, unmarried, earning a wage – that's me.
I work here.

[Leaning against the wall]

Have you accepted me as a narrator by now? You are following me. You are after all in my place, standing on my bed, on my table, my sofa, my book shelf, standing in my view. My labour, I am selling it here. Who has lived in this room before?

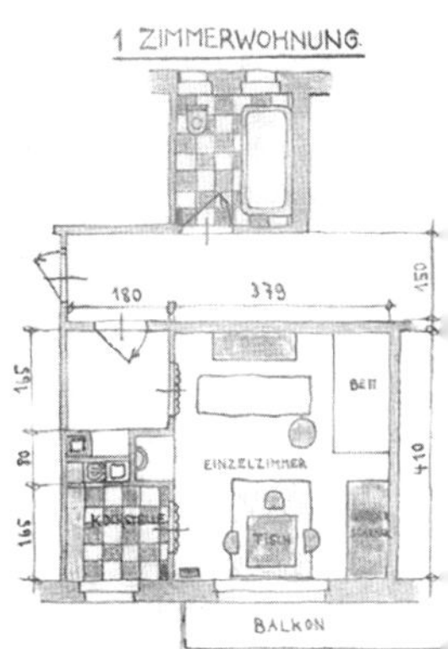

Women, unmarried, earning a wage. What were their names?

'Maria Anna Abel-Auer, Simone Natural, Matilde Lejeune-Jehle…'

What do you read in these names? They have also been domesticated.

They belonged to travelling people, or were given to them. We don't know. This was also eliminated. What is told is the story of a house, a farm. This name appears proper and clean. What else? My grandfather was an engineer, not far from here. Turbines, technologies for progress and white supremacy. Most of the others: untraceable, in the name and the archive that this name could be.

[From behind the wall a record plays]

'My first letter is double-u. I've never been known. I'm not in your history, your heart or your soul. Your paintings and pictures don't show my real face. You cut me and wrap me in ribbons and lace.'

What is important in all this is who took care of whom, who is taking care of the ways in which we can see. Through which histories and forms of authority do we tell each other who we can be.

Integration too is a special performance of translation. We do not want to perform it anymore. What has exile got to do with how women were living and working in the 1930s on both sides of the river here.

Everything is connected, therefore I tell everything
at once.

At the train station in Chiasso, between Milan and   Projection off
Zurich, the train stops, even if it is not indicated on
the schedule. The carriage is almost empty. Nobody
talks. Even the border police keep quiet, as they
pass along the passengers asking for papers, doing
their own racial profiling, reconstructing borders
that were supposed to be abandoned with the independence of former colonies and most recently with
the Schengen agreement. Soon there will be a ferry,
a direct connection from Tunis to Lake Zurich, in
both directions and for free.

Looking from the Material Testing Institute
towards the shipbuilding, both buildings part of
Escher Wyss Machine Works.

[Reading descriptions as found in the Escher Wyss archive]

'Chemical, physical and hydraulic labor of the Material
Testing Institute of Escher Wyss, Zurich 1945'

'Section "Research" (diapositives)'

'The work of the proficiency bureau'

'Atatürk, information for the installation team 1986'

'Swiss shipping on the seas'

'The history of waterways corrections'

'Retouches and clichés of photos and schemes'

'Zurich builds for those forgotten'

'Heat-resistant steels, works by the Material Testing Institute'

'Lectures by Dr. C. Keller for Escher Wyss in Minas Gerais Brasil'

'Welfare house'

'New laboratory for thermal turbo-machines'

'Agreements with the Sulzer brothers in Winterthur'

'Escher Wyss product development'

'Reports on factory visits'

'Red flyers'

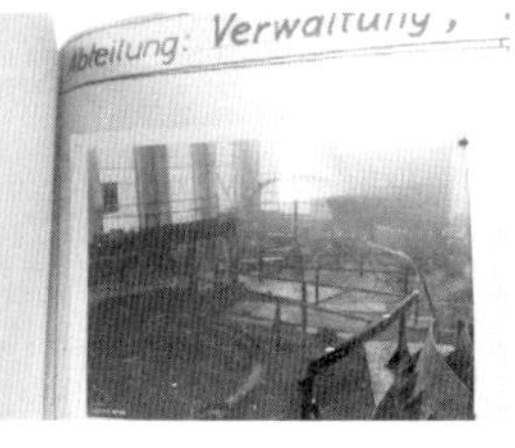

Turning pages in the archives of Escher Wyss, looking at what has been tested in this Material Testing Institute, which proofs of progress, which formations of a colonised world, by chance – or maybe not – I came across a small picture amongst many:

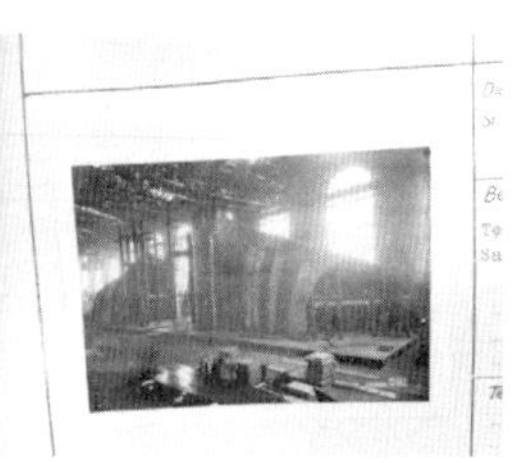

After pictures documenting the construction of the Aswan dam, sheets and notes on the exchange of knowledge and gifts with German submarine manufacturers during World War Two, appears a worker or a gaffer, portrayed with some blank grenades on a pallet.

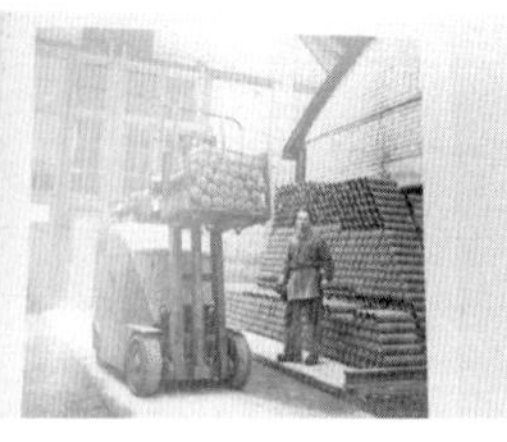

Like potatoes. In the way that everything ends up piled up on a pallet in this archive of a war without war.

[Turning around, speaking towards the front wall of the cube, which separates the gallery storage from the exhibition space]

What is this space that no one sees? Is it private or shared?

[Knocking on the cube's front wall]

Are there people with uncertain residency status being hosted here, or is it about private property?

[Behind the wall a record plays]

'You called me Jacky, I call you Athena, sitting in the creamery, laughing at the paper heads we made...'

[Song fades out]

Whose dress are you wearing?

[Turning around, towards the listeners]

I read: 'Whose dream are you bearing?' This happened, after I had been locked in my room with fever for five days. Alone with myself, that is to say: language. When the sun was shining outside, I also felt better in there.

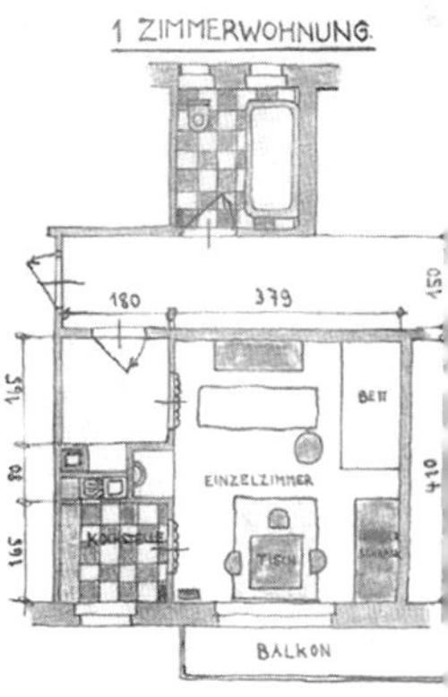

I don't know, for example, where the stove was placed in this room. Who had been living here before me? I know that it has always been women. Un-married, earning a wage.

[Taking a seat on the empty equipment box]

The archive of the Housing Cooperative of Working Women, a loose collection of newspaper clippings, annual reports and photographs:

'Residential home for working women, 1925: "Special attention is given to interior design. Practical measures diminish the amount of housework. Three projects were presented to the assembly of delegates: project A is the cheapest and has the character of an asylum. The living spaces are being rented out individually, the side rooms are for common use, meals are consumed together." Der öffentliche Dienst, Nummer 29, 1947.'

'The housing shortage and single women: "Single women are not allowed in most cities to rent an apartment alone – even though no difference is made between subletting a room and renting an apartment." Volksrecht, Stadt Zürich, April 20, 1951.'

'Epitaph to Agnes Robmann: "The small groups of women in the party banded together into women groups, and Agnes Robmann was the leading chairwoman. She introduced us to political life. Not an easy task. Most women – just as today – did not have any kind of political rights? Thanks to Agnes Robmann we have the daily page 'Narrated Lives' [Erzähltes Leben] with our own editor in the newspaper 'Political Rights' [Volksrecht]. It is expandable. Now it's our turn, the comrades of tomorrow." Unspecified newspaper snippet, 1951.'

Agnes Robmann. Finally a name. How did Agnes Robmann live, what did she fight for, when fighting for women's rights. In the former industrial area Binz there is a small path named after her.

In a name, in your name –

The houses have been restored, but not the ways of living. The houses restored in a way they never were before. The houses have been reconstructed, new-built sceneries looking old in a nice way, new-built history looking old in the right and straight way. Somehow real, somehow true. Industrial history has been torn down or renovated, in an untouchable way. An authorised narrative, untouchable, unless you outbid other investors.

'And then she says they can't be owned.'

As the translator is translating, the woman says that language has been taken away from her. The inter-linking of words. That what she felt well in has been taken away. She also says that she doesn't like the word 'home', because it has been contaminated so strongly by the ideals of the settled: the nuclear family, the smallest unit of the nation state, of bourgeois society and its claims of ownership on lives and grounds, values and representation, and its violent solutions for dealing with fights and difference – domestication, integration, or silencing indifference.

'Monsieur, Le Commissaire aux Droits de l'Homme, a pris connaissance de votre communication et m'a chargée de vous répondre.'

[Radio fades out]

It is language, she says, that carries her with it. Now that she cannot use it anymore, she feels lost and disconnected. Full and heavy with words and incomplete sentences that do no longer find a public. We don't know if there was a reception here. If one of the women was already here, when the men started their working day in the Material Testing Institute. We know that this building will stay, because it is protected. Only the view will be changed. The view is being changed right now, torn down or renovated, restored back to a way it never was. Even the view is being domesticated.

The performance could take place anywhere. The performance has no fixed home, and this is what interests her most, Esther Ferrer writes.

[Taking off the masks and hanging them where before the projection was]

Second projection
in the back goes on

no easy adapt!

  profit *(welcome) de transit*°

a. ⊠

a.   agir

It's not easy to adapt / To this, to this situation, to this society, to this language / We do not want to adapt / we do not want to be integrated, to be domesticated / Not our bodies, not our language, not our everyday actions / not our thoughts and how they move / What we want are equal possibilities / No matter where we come from and where we go to / For some it's only the profit that makes a welcome. For some the welcome means a welcome to transit.

In this case the welcome is only a welcome to the onward journey. Zur Durchreise.

A: Do something, say something, say what you think, resist

A for Agir: Act

[Walking off, into the storage space behind the exhibtion wall]

How many masks do you wear today?

'You called me Jacky, I call you Athena, sitting in the cream okey, laughing at the paper heads we made. A white sea gull, a boarding house, sitting round the table, your sister, brother, mother, little girl...'

Notes

The Housing Cooperative of Working Women (Baugenossenscha Berufstätiger Frauen Zürich) was set up because women were not allowed to rent alone. If they did manage to do so, they were often suspected of being a sex worker. The new heavy metal industries (among others) on the other hand offered women jobs that guaranteed them a legal income to rent and live alone. Similar housing initiatives existed in Basel and Vienna at that time. The Housing Cooperative for Working Women was initiated by women who were educated as commercial assistants (Kaufmännische Angestellte), the architect Lux Guyer planned the first of the buildings with several communal spaces, including an alcohol free restaurant. The apartments were though promoted as mini homes and adjusted according to bourgeois concepts – single apartments that would go along with middle-class ideals of one's own home.

Escher Wyss Machine Works (Maschinenfabrik) was a major industrial enterprise in Zurich, whose buildings are still being torn down or restored today. The transformation of the former industrial district of which the Escher Wyss area is part of, is the subject of political debates on urban development and migration politics. The main actors are housing cooperatives, city offcials, real-estate speculators and banks, as well as server farms, empty office buildings, squatters, financial institutes, schools, artists and arts organizations.

Text references

– Cristina Peri Rossi, *State of Exile*, City Lights Publishers, San Francisco 2008
– Christian Koller, *Vor 75 Jahren entstand das rote Zürich*, in 'Rote Revue: Zeitschrift für Politik, Wirtschaft und Kultur', 2003
– Articles and documents collected by the Housing Cooperative of Working Women
– Maggie Andrews, *Domesticating the Airwaves. Broadcasting, Domesticity and Femininity, Bloomsbury*, London 2012
– Rosa Luxemburg, *Die Akkumulation des Kapitals. Ein Beitrag zur ökonomischen Erklärung des Imperialismus* (1912), in *Gesammelte Werke Band 5. Ökonomische Schriften*, Dietz Verlag, East Berlin 1975
– Esther Ferrer, *Utopía y Performance*, for the seminar 'L'abri et l'utopie' at the Institute of Higher Artistic Studies, Paris 2017
– Gosteli–Stiftung Archiv zur Geschichte der schweizerischen Frauenbewegung (Archive about the history of women's movements in Switzerland)
– Letter by the European Council in Strasbourg answering the Tayad Komitee Schweiz, November 14, 2014: 'Estemmed, the Commissioner for Human Rights has taken notice of your letter and told me to respond to you...'
– Lygia Clark, *Are we domesticated?*, 1968. 'If I was younger I would do politics, but I am too much at ease, too integrated'

Sound references

– Etel Adnan, recorded interviews and readings found on eteladnan.com
– *Who am I?* by The Fates, in 'Furia', LP 1985
– *You Called me Jacky* by Les Reines Prochaines, in 'Lob Ehre Ruhm Dank', LP 1983

An abandoned border checkpoint between Basel and France, green fields, an empty synagogue, an art space in a former sewing factory. After the agreements on the free movements of persons within Europe have been signed, the checkpoints are silently replaced by an invisible line. A border line remains, for some in memory, for many in reality.

A recorded description on headphones accompanies the listeners while leaving the former factory space, taking them along this and other invisible lines. The trilingual text is based on newspaper reports, online research and mailing lists. Each language follows a slightly different path.

The field recordings were made during work breaks on the park above the collections at Museum Rietberg in Zurich. The typeface in this text highlights the three different languages.

Exhibition hall, former industrial space	[Sound of steps on a field]

Une promenade le long des mots. En trois langues. Je suis ton audioguide. Les audioguides t'invitent à faire des promenades: à te promener, à te promener dans une image, une image de promenade. Eine Audiotour entlang von Worten gehen. *Jusqu'à la frontière, à la bordure de l'image, jusqu'à l'horizon.* **What words do we want to describe, invent and comment on this tour?** Durch eine Landschaft aus bestehenden Worten gehen. **In which words may I guide you through?**

Quelle langue parlez-vous? D'où venez-vous ? Noch wissen wir nicht was und in welche Richtung wir queren. *Je te prie, en plusieurs langues de bien vouloir me suivre.* **To involve the possibility of not** excluding too many people? Let's also choose imagination, a language of one's own.

[Sound of chalk on a board, drawing a line from left to right]

Let's begin this walk with a first step. With a step to the right. On the chalkboard I prepared a drawing for you. Eine Wandtafel mit einer Silhouette. *Blanc sur noir, un chemin esquissé, le pourtour d'un corps, d'un mot, d'une région.* **It shows what kind of walk we will do:** *Une figure de mots.*

In any case the board can be washed out and there won't be any sign left. Nichts würde mehr darauf hinweisen, was wir vorhaben zu tun.

Have a look at the chalkboard.

Try to remember our route by heart. Simple signs and symbols were used to draw that line – Another blurry line.

Une ligne floue. Une ligne étendue par des corps contrôlant d'autres corps les traversant. **A line extended by bodies controlling other bodies crossing it. Crossing without seeing what.** *Les croisant sans ne rien voir.*

Watch the chalkboard closely. Essaie de t'en souvenir par coeur.

Walking around in the factory

[Factory sounds, machines running, of a big empty hall]

Commence à te balader dans l'espace. Dans l'exposition. Tu peux à tout moment revenir. Revenir jeter un coup d'oeil au tableau noir. **A map showing a route, a river, a body's outside.**

Probably used for lessons in Geography. Mensch und Umwelt sei der Name des Unterrichts.

The lesson hasn't started yet, the teacher didn't enter the room. He's a bit late today. *La leçon n'a pas encore commencé. Aujourd'hui le professeur est un peu en retard.*

Die Lehrerin kommt möglicherweise nicht. Es wird gesagt sie arbeite im Untergrund, es wird auch gesagt sie arbeite für die Staatssicherheit, es wird auf jeden Fall gesagt sie bringe den Kindern die falsche Geschichte bei. **The concept of history, as something written down in books.**

Die Geschichte neu und anders schreiben, um auf jene zu verweisen, die darin fehlen. *Écrire une histoire nouvelle et autre faisant apparaître ceux qui en sont absent.* **When rewriting history, let's add blank pages for everything that cannot be told. For all the ones that had to die because of what they had to say.** Leere Seiten für all jene, die wir weiterhin nicht hören.

Qu'est-ce que tu portes? **Good shoes? A jogging dress? Tight jeans, an old jumper and a loose jacket, just as the other young artists around you?**

Marche lentement dans la fabrique. Observe ce qui peut t'intéresser: **The artworks, the shed-ceiling, the imprints of the machines on the floor.**

At least try to pretend.

We haven't been tought how to read maps yet and the teacher won't make it to see his class today. Nobody asks. The students just sit and read, the silence is marking a general fear.

Leaving
the factory

**I will explain this piece to you, describing what
you see and how you can proceed. A space to move
– dressed up as an audio tour.**

Une pomme, un papier et à pied. **Take an apple,
take a chalk and walk.**

[Sound of a door]

Wir gehen nun.Vollkommen gewöhnlich gehen wir
durch die Tür, so wie alle vollkommen gewöhnlich
durch die Tür gehen, über die man später sagen
wird, dass man etwas geahnt hätte an jenem Morgen,
Nachmittag, Abend, dass man geahnt hätte, dass sie
nicht mehr zurückkehren würden. **People are watching you, yes they do. It's just a normal art venue.**

A few instructions. Eine kleine Einleitung, Anleitung
zur Begleitung. *Quelques instructions.* **I would like
to invite you to cross a border, to cross something
like an invisible line as part of this piece.**

Geh auf den kleinen Vorplatz der Fabrik.

*Vas lentement en direction des boîtes aux lettres à
l'entrée de la fabrique. Arrête-toi de temps à autre
et observe-la comme si tu imaginais son histoire.*
**Did you know they produced yarn in this area –
and also in here?** *On a exporté des tissues. On a
échanché ces tissues contre des esclaves. On a exploité
les esclaves dans les plantations, dans les colonies.
Maintenant on échange de la culture dans ces salles.*

**It's art that speaks a language of exchange, of open
borders – they say. The principle of colonisation by
education and cultural exchange.** *On ouvre les
frontières dans les mots et au nom de l'art, pour ceux
avec un privilège.*

Routes of transfer, of transgress, of exchange – seem to be deeply inscribed into whom we reach when we speak.

La frontière était pour la construction de l'usine un bon argument. Zollabgaben, sind der Grund, dass die Fabrik seit rund 100 Jahren auf dieser Seite der Grenze steht und nicht dort.

Tu te trouves en dehors, et peut-être qu'il fait déjà nuit. N'utilise pas de lampe, la carte est dans ta tête. Ton coeur bat plus fort. Commence à marcher autour du bâtiment calmement et lentement.

Walking towards the centre of the village

[Steps on asphalt]

Passe vers les boîtes aux lettre colorées en direction du centre du village. Entlang einer unsichtbaren Linie gehen. **Let's walk along such a line.** *En jouant à l'amateur d'art.* **Pretend to be a visitor of an art-show. An art show that speaks about a region. A region inviting you to cross.**

To cross the rivers and fields, to enter and leave, the halls of thoughts and representation. Creating a field of exchange – for whom? *Pour quoi?* **For you?** *Pour toi? Pour moi?* **For me?**

Geh einfach weiter, auf dieser Strasse vor dir, vor deinem inneren Auge, ein gewöhnliches Wohnquartier. **Follow the street, the fabric seems already far, we are about to leave.**

[Sounds of airplanes]

Les avions traversent le ciel. Siehst du die Flugzeuge über uns? **How strong are your arms? Could you** hold on to the feet of a bird to be carried away to another play?

Pretend to be on a Sunday walk. Über den lokalen Schrottplatz gehen.

Returning to the industrial zone of Hégenheim

Autrefois on construisait les usines à Hégenheim – près de la frontière, à cause de la frontière. Aujourd'hui on construit les usines à Bâle, à cause de la frontière et près de la frontière.

Go ahead, continue. Pass that small round house and enter the industrial zone of the town. It's a very small area compared to the one on the other side of the border. *Pas à pas,* **guiding you over – from here to there. From nowhere to an other empty scene.**

Une scène qui n'existe pas. Une existence qui n'existe pas et n'existera pas. Einen Dokumentarfilm drehen, über das was wir gerne sähen.

It's not far, it's an easy walk. *C'est simplement une promenade.*

Secrets and words are driving you. Where do you come from? You and your words. Repeating the words and the ways and the plays. *Tu marches à travers la petite zone industrielle d'Hégenheim. Devant toi se trouve maintenant un champ. Allons-y lentement.* Am Ende des Ackers siehst du keine Grenze, sondern den Beginn einer Industrie.

Crossing the field   [Steps on a field in winter]

Tu es surveillé. Von oben von hinten, von vorne sieht man dich. Über ein matschiges, über ein gefrohrenes Feld im Grenzbebiet gehen. **You are being watched while walking with that audio guide. From one art venue to another.** Worte sind es, die dazu beitragen, dass wir migrieren.

Standing on
the border line

[Sound of breathing]

Je suis heureuse de voir que ton passeur a décidé de te donner un look de cycliste, roulant pour un tour du dimanche, traversant les champs gelés et les bois. **The field is frozen, keep walking.**

[Science fiction sounds]

A line clearly inscribed: into landscape, into images, into memory. Lines used to mark the border of another world – we have been told. *Cette ligne est décrite comme verte ou bleue, brune ou blanche.* **Let's describe it as invisible and blurry.** *Décrivons cette ligne comme invisible et floue.*

What are we trying to reach? Hidden places, places named but out of sight? Orte, die wir aus Erzählungen kennen.

Green borders, invisible lines. They seem to be there to describe what can not be articulated or represented.

Gemeinsam über die grüne Grenze gehen. *Une ligne imaginaire, floue et bien protégée. Celle qui est parfois utilisée comme un argument. Comme un lieu passionnant où les pays et les cultures se rencontrent. La même frontière qui justifie: qui à le droit de se déplacer sur un territoire et qui ne l'a pas. Qui est invité à quel échange et qui ne l'est pas. Qui ne vas pas être capable de prendre part à quelconque échange.*

Are you invited to this exchange? In wessen Namen lassen Sie sich über die Grenze führen? Worte migrieren. *Les mots vous guident.*

'Les passeurs donnent des cartes à leurs clients': Schlepper gäben ihren Klienten und Klientinnen Karten mit auf den Weg, der sich für sie über die Grüne Grenze legt. Auf ihren Weg durch die Wälder, Gärten, Äcker, Wiesen und Industriezonen.

The border: a mental concept of openness, of control, of fear, of history, of future, constructing differences.

An adjective for or against exchange. Exchange of human bodies. Human working power. Exchange of culture, of art works, of art workers.

Allez au fil des mots de l'autre côté de la frontière. Et lorsque quelqu'un vous demande d'où et pourquoi – dann antworte, man habe dir die Sprache genommen, die Möglichkeit zu artikulieren. Bist du in diesem Moment eine Sans Papier, oder eine Reisende mit wechselnden Namen? **You can use my name, I don't mind.**

The factory is old. How come you are interested in this place? They might say. *Est-ce que vous parlez français? Quel est votre nom?* **Do People only die if we hear them cry? What kind of exile are you trying to reach?**

Alleine mit einer Karte in der Hand auf der grünen Grenze stehen. **Have you learned how to read? How to read a map? A map of imagination?**

[Steps approaching]

Parlez-vous Français? Sprechen sie Deutsch, sprechen Sie?

On the other side of the border

Ich frage nach dem Bus, nach dem Bus von hier nach weiter. Klettern Sie einfach über den Haag, sagt eine Passantin.

Nous avons traversé la frontière, et nous avons laissé derrière des silhouettes, maintenant nous sommes là.

Und nun? **Invention of a new identity, a reason to stay? Keep on walking to see another exhibition.** Das Buch ist frisch gepresst, seine Autorin längst im Exil. In welchem, in diesem, das wir ihr nicht geben? **Please walk in any name, cross the border again and again. To move, to move words, ideas and bodies from here to there.**

Have you already started crossing the street? Walking back to the factory? Ich habe das Gefühl dich verloren zu haben, ihre Aufmerksamkeit, die Erinnerung, den Wegbeschrieb. **Let's go back to the start and let's try a little bit later again.**

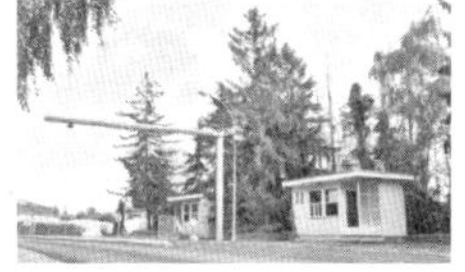

A federal museum in the Ticino countryside, south of the Alps with a view of the border towards Italy. White plaster models for statues and monuments. The Gotthard base tunnel is opened shortly beforehand. Who cleans here at night invisibly? Whose work is it to keep the statues as white as can be, representing male and female role models for the ideas of the modern nation state? Two climbers, alone at night in the museum.

A and B, a performer and someone following with a broken arm, illuminating the scene with a small beamer. The audience moving among the performers in alternating circles. Three friends are speaking the four voices in Italian (Offstage, Comment, Night Worker and Desolation), all with a slightly different accent in their wording, which may or may not point towards a first or second generation experience of work migration.

All voices are pre-recorded and played back through the museum's ceiling speakers; therefore the typeface is plane throughout the entire text.

[Ground floor, hall , in front of the plaster model La Desolazione (Desolation). Figure A sits on a pedestal, waiting. Different plastic bags full of talcum powder are arranged in front of her. Ambient sound: a gathering thunderstorm]

[Playing *Furia* by the Fates]

'My first letter is double-u. I've never been known. I'm not in your history, your heart or your soul. Your paintings and pictures don't show my real face. You cut me and wrap me in ribbons and lace…'

[Figure A places the pedestal in front of the statue Desolation, by tipping it over]

'Your poets disguise me in mystery and sin. Desired is my flesh, buxom and slim. Your words can't describe the person I am…'

[Figure B sits in a corner]

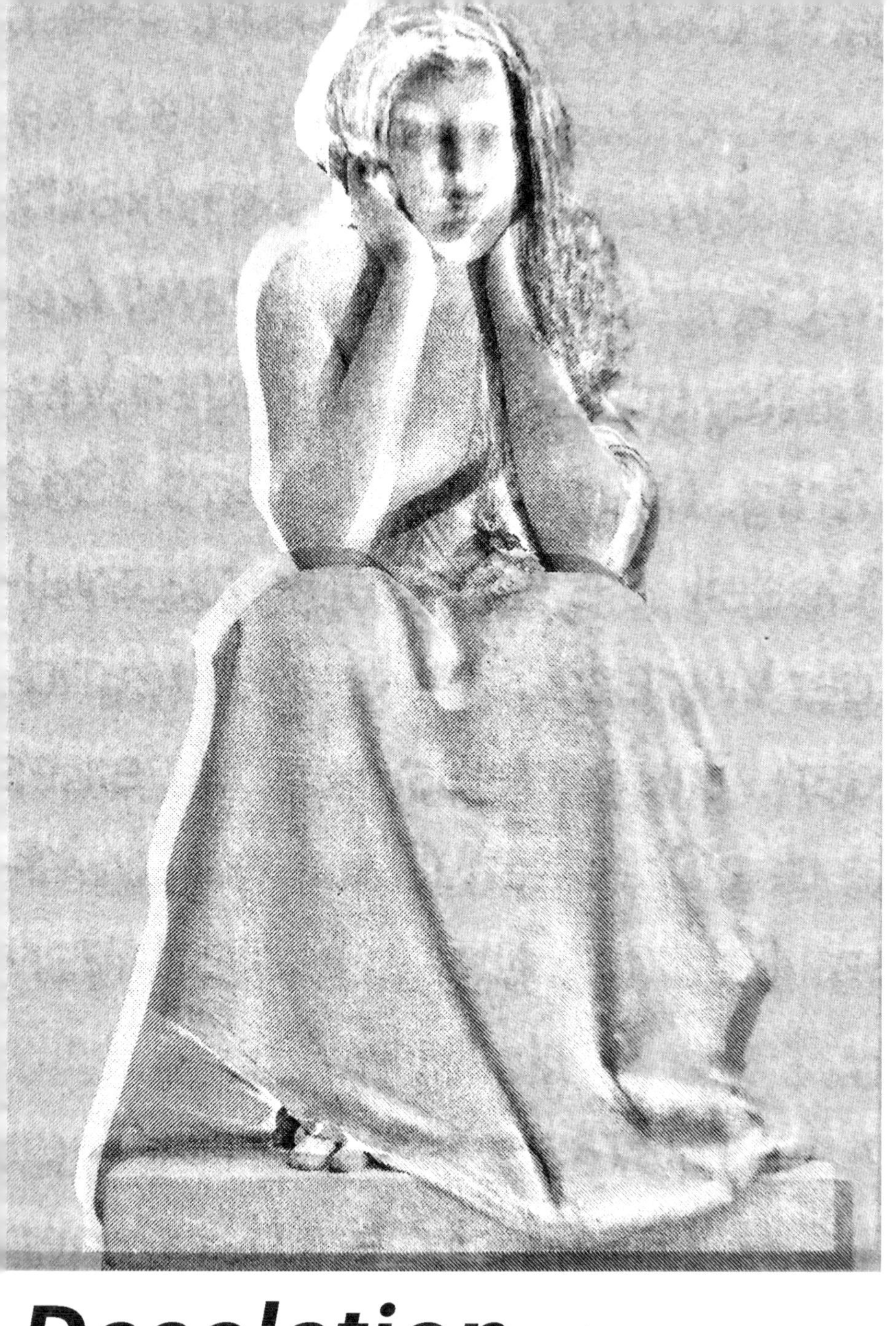

Desolation

Offstage voice   First passage through history.

[Figure A sits on a pedestal in front of the plaster model Desolation, imitating its pose]

Offstage voice   Desolation.

[Figure B projects on the statue the subtitle Desolation]

Offstage voice   You can see Italy from here. The refugees are waiting for a transit, a passage. The Gotthard base tunnel has yet to become fully operational. At the border in Chiasso, they stop the buses. Those who travel by bus are suspect. Those who travel cheaply are suspect. Having to declare an identity, even if there is nothing else to declare. The real one and the fake one, a first name and a family name, a nationality, a face that goes with the picture, the colour of your skin.

Comment   The woman next to me in the halted bus tells me she has waited years for this new train connection. For many years, she has been commuting from Zurich to Milan every weekend, for her private life. And late every Sunday evening, she travels back to Zurich from Milan, for work on Monday morning.

Offstage voice   In the hope of work. For work on Monday morning, people head north, after the North has exploited their South. From the south of the South, from the South to the north of the South, to the North, to the north of the North.

Comment   In the train, the border police go through the wagons faster. They can't let the train wait like a bus – after all, there is still a first class on the train. The border police have to go about their work quickly, since this border has been nominally abolished. They don't bother to check each passenger's passport, but pick out their suspects promptly, depending on the colour of your skin.

Offstage voice   This blossoming garden, the immaculate white of the statues – not everyone is allowed to see this paradise of pure conscience, this fiction from a time long past.

Comment   Only very few apply for asylum. Most migrants want to pass through, so that they might arrive – by the time they reach maturity – in a country that welcomes them.

[Figure B moves the projection back and forth between the plaster model and the performer]

Woman night worker   Today, I will disrupt the work of reproduction. Today, I will be an interruption.

[Figure A rolls up the sleeves of its shirt, takes a bag with talcum powder and brings it over to the next room, under the equestrian plaster model]

Woman night worker   I get up at five am and put a pot of water on the stove. Today, I will disrupt the work of reproduction, in an underpaid way, as is apparently the norm for reproductive labour.

Desolation   The time in which I live does not yet recognise reproductive labour as work, but someone is getting it done.

[In front of the equestrian plaster model, Figure A puts talcum powder on her hands. Figure B moves the projection along with what is being said]

Offstage voice   A man on horseback in an upright position, with a plain, straight gaze, staring straight ahead. To have to get up on the pedestal to look him in the eye – this is not how it was intended. The man keeps his eyes steadily on the horizon, a man with a vision, and he has a name, too. He – that is, a man, a horse and a pedestal – are part of the cultural heritage, as the website of this federal museum indicates. It goes almost like this: this country, as a nation, is what he left behind.

Comment   A monumental sculpture is one that has left the domestic environment of villas and palaces. It is exhibited on a plaza or an otherwise well-frequented place in a village or city, so it can be publicly viewed, and thus serves a representative function for the larger public.

[Figure A walks back to Desolation]

Comment   It is a silent message that will never run away, until the regime changes. Sometimes, a monumental sculpture is erected on a historic location deemed worthy to be remembered. Location, monument, and history books share the same narrative, creating authenticity, creating a reality that is affective.

Offstage voice   Second passage through history.

[Figure A sits on a pedestal in front of Desolation, imitating its pose]

Offstage voice   Lost in desolation for 166 years.

[Figure A projects the subtitle 'Lost in desolation for 166 years']

Offstage voice   Dreams are valid in only one direction, as the Swiss Federal Railways SBB writes on its blog about the Gotthard base tunnel: 'Making the journey from the grey north to the blue skies of the south has long been the dream of many people […]. Celebrations were held in honour of this new structure, which, to this day, is still considered an outstanding feat of engineering and surveying, as well as a masterpiece of railway construction.' A tour de force that forces its way through the rock and conquers every obstacle, a vision of absolute control over the landscape, implemented by returnees from the colonies.

Comment   Bypass Napoleon's Continental Blockade for cotton from the Americas – cotton, after all, could be planted in the two Sicilies – and gain access to the southern ports. Silent colonialism has a tradition.

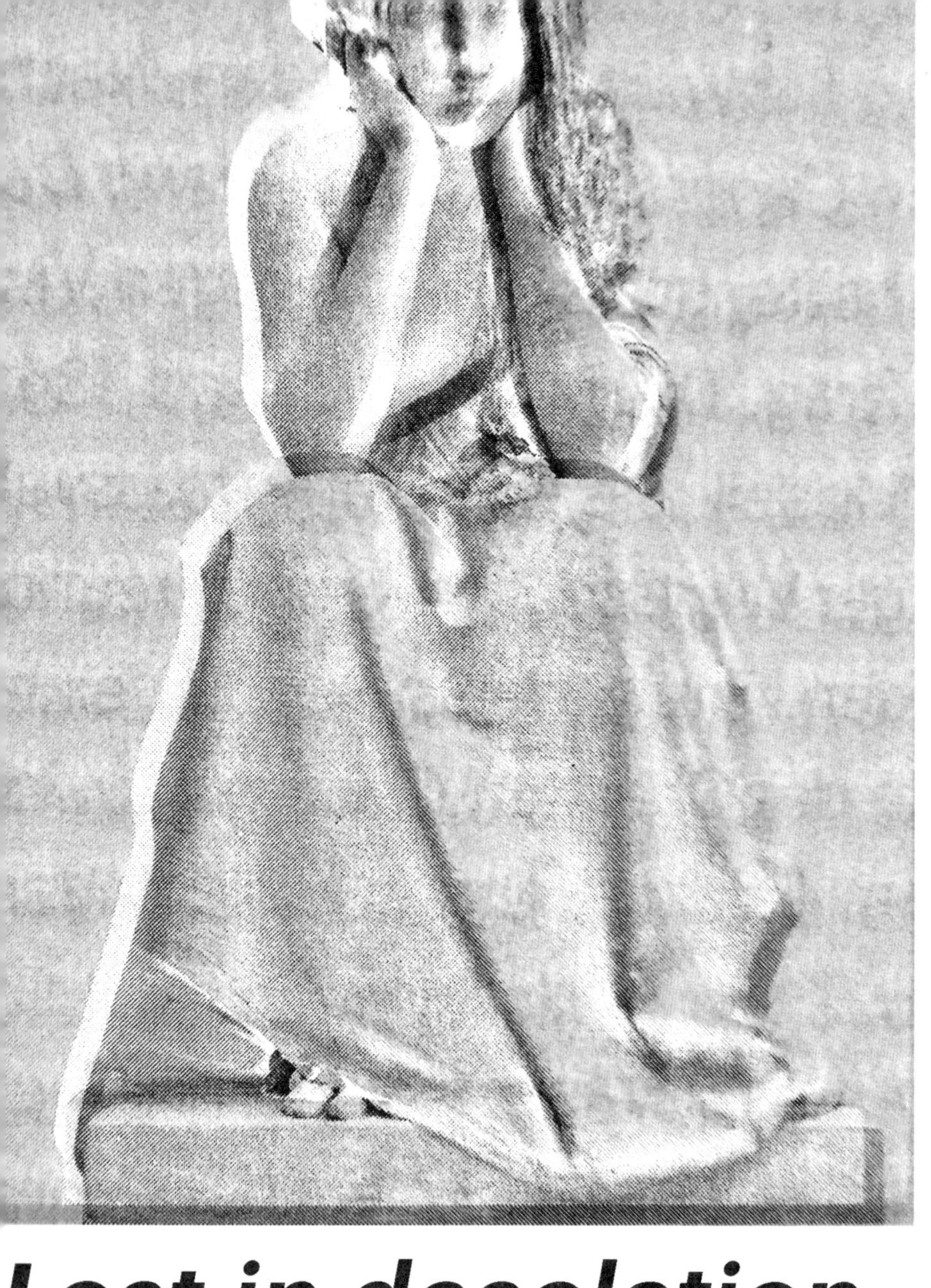

Lost in desolation for 166 years

Offstage voice   Or, as the Swiss Federal Council declared this summer at the inauguration of the new Gotthard base tunnel, in an official video message to a grandstand full of men in grey suits, and in tribute to Swiss railway magnates Favre and Escher: 'With the construction of the century we build on the pioneering achievements of our ancestors. People and goods can now move faster. Cities like Stuttgart, Zurich, Lugano and Milan are linked much better. With the Gotthard Base Tunnel we bring together people and nations and national economies.'

Comment   Did you grow up without a father most of the time, too, because he had to look for work in some other country?

Offstage voice   Not that the fathers are necessarily so important, just so we know who the Swiss Federal Council is talking about here.

Desolation   And who forgot to instruct the border police to cooperate with this officially announced and instituted speed-up of connections, people and goods?

Woman night worker   Today, I will disrupt the work of reproduction. Today, I will be an interruption. I get up at six am and put the kettle on.

[Figure A walks among the audience and in front of the monument Vittime del Lavoro (The Victims of Labour), puts talcum powder on its entire arms up to the elbows]

Offstage voice   Victims of labour
Victims of the Inquisition
Victims of capital
Victims of imperialism
Victims of the new bourgeoisie
Victims of heteronormativity
Victims of patriarchy
Victims of the history of representation

>   Victims of earth's gravity
>   Victims of passion
>   Victims of colonial exploitation
>   Victims of unilateral border regimes

[Figure A goes back to its starting point, in front of Desolation]

Comment   Leaving behind the nation state, this crazy fantasy, which was available to only a few. The whole patriarchal institution, its gender roles, the morals of the bourgeoisie – leaving it all behind. Leaving behind reproductive labour. Leaving behind existing gender hierarchies.

Offstage voice   Third passage through history.

[Figure A imitates the pose of Desolation]

Offstage voice   Not everyone is assigned a name. Those who do not have a name represent something else, an allegory in this case.

Desolation   They say I am lost in desolation, in despair, when all I do is think.

Comment   Apparently, allegories are almost always female because woman are, supposedly, outside of economic and military competition.

Desolation   They made me a woman. So that I wouldn't pose a threat to power. Why else would it be necessary to categorize me, to gender my facial features, my wig, my costume? To force me into the gender binary. My surface is white, white plaster. Who could have been my model?

[Figure A does some warm ups, talcum powder on arms and legs]

Desolation   They made me like a photographic image, but as a sculpture. My face is carved in innocence in such a naturalistic, veristic way, the long hair scattered over the hand where my chin is resting. As a material, I am transitive and intransitive at the same time. This is the power of the allegory.

Offstage voice   A young person with long hair sits on a metal beam, thinking.

[Figure B projects the subtitle 'A young person with long hair sits on a metal beam, thinking']

Woman night worker   Today, I will disrupt the work of reproduction. Today, I will be an interruption. At 7:30 am I am awake and already in the streetcar. Today, I will disrupt the work of reproduction – as a part of my reproductive labour.

[Figure A puts talcum powder on its body, goes over to the equestrian plaster model, stands directly in front of it. Figure B follows the performer, with the projection as a source of light]

Offstage voice   A man on horseback in an upright position, with a plain, straight gaze, staring straight ahead.

Woman night worker   I have to climb up on his pedestal to look him in the eye, so high up on his horse he is – but this is not how it was intended.

Offstage voice   You said that already.

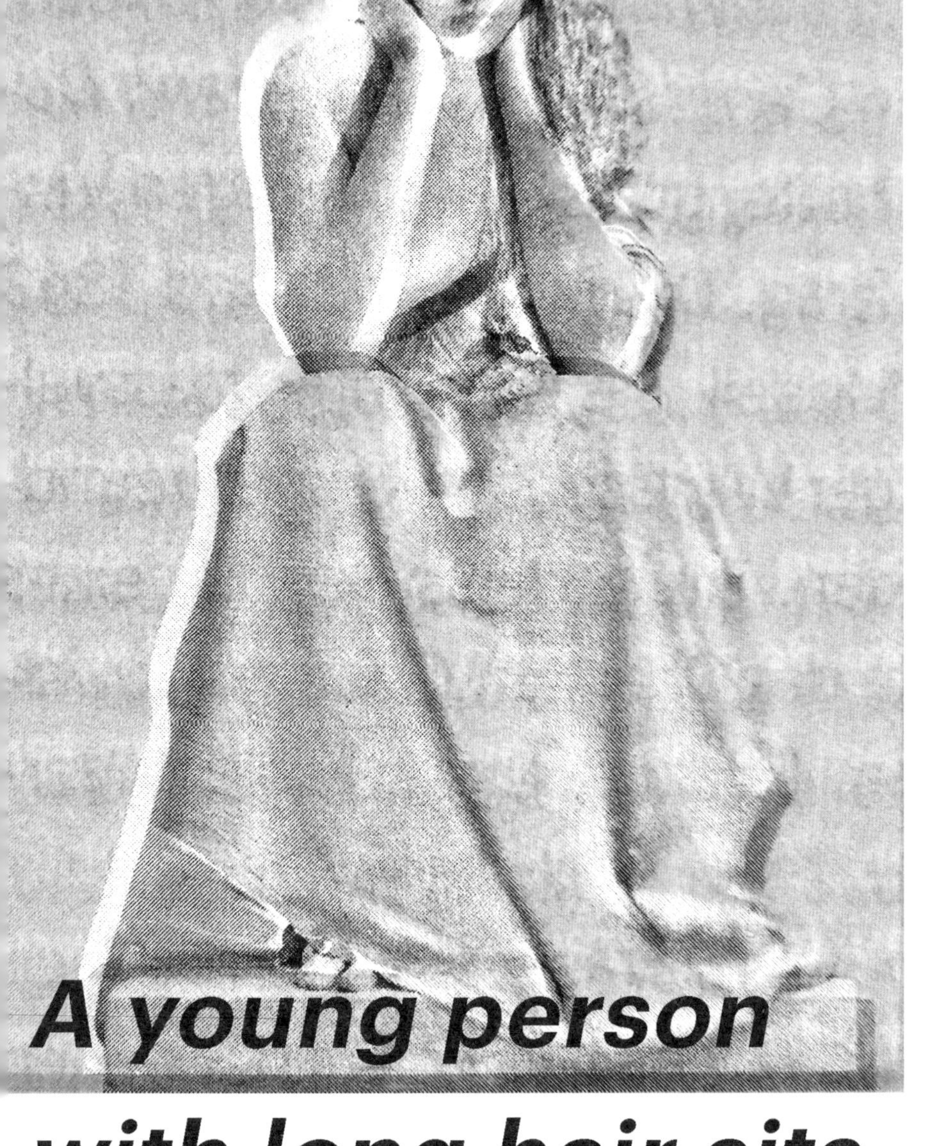

**A young person with long hair sits on a metal beam, thinking

Woman night worker   It's not so easy, the plaster has really been re-stored well. The history of the *white* men is being preserved so well here that people like me have no way of attaching ourselves to it.

[Figure B takes the lead with the projection. Figure A goes to the next room, full of allegorical models. Stops in front of the plaster model Italy Grateful to France]

Offstage voice   Doleful harmony
Liberty
The uprising
The two queens
Springtime/Flora
Justitia
Morning prayer
Helvetia
Italy Grateful to France
Elena Kisses Joséphine!

Comment   Two women who kiss each other!

Offstage voice   Italy shows its gratitude to France with a kiss. It's surprising that the two women like each other so much, across language barriers! And this in a time when it was certainly very much against the law, the love between women. A love that starts with desire, whereas bourgeois love represents reproduction, the reproduction of the species.

Comment   Otherwise, the statues are all very isolated, only the kids are allowed to play in eternity.

[Figure A goes back to the equestrian statue]

Woman night worker   To get up every morning and wash clothes,
wash the kids, wash the floors.

Comment   I am talking about a kind of work that takes
place at home.

[Figure A walks around the equestrian statue. Figure B uses the light from the projection to illuminate the different plaster statues and busts of important historic figures that are arranged around the equestrian statue]

Comment   The village fountain
The sink
The washing machine
The ironing board
The washing line
The dryer
The slap in the face
The slap back
The marital duty
The refusal of the marital duty
The ear that listens and understands
The lowered gaze
The passage of air
The double-standards
The soup pot
The steamer
The broom
The vacuum cleaner
The diaper
The cold compress
The mash
The disinfectant
The way to school
The way to the doctor

Availability
The cold hand on a feverish forehead
The quick call to ask how it's going
A reminder of what the other person said
Empathy or radical relatedness, the
politicized form of empathy

[Figure A goes back to Desolation]

Offstage voice Fourth passage through history.

[Figure A sits on a pedestal in front of the plaster statue Desolation, imitating its pose]

Woman night worker A woman sits on a metal beam modelling for a tombstone statue, thinking, since posing as a model is boring and doesn't pay well.

[Figure B projects the subtitle 'A woman sits on a metal beam modeling for a tombstone statue, thinking, since posing as a model is boring and doesn't pay well']

Offstage voice This hall would be full of sculptures if they had paid tribute to the working folks. If they had paid tribute to the women, the elderly, and the poor. But would the Swiss Confederation care to preserve this museum if it told the story of a country full of peddlers and vagrants, thus the story of those who could be a reminder that it was not so long ago that the founding of the nation state made it necessary to domesticate the people, to assign them a place of residence and of origin, to take away their children and prohibit their journeying way of life? Even if the pressure to settle down and assimilate started even earlier in Central Europe.

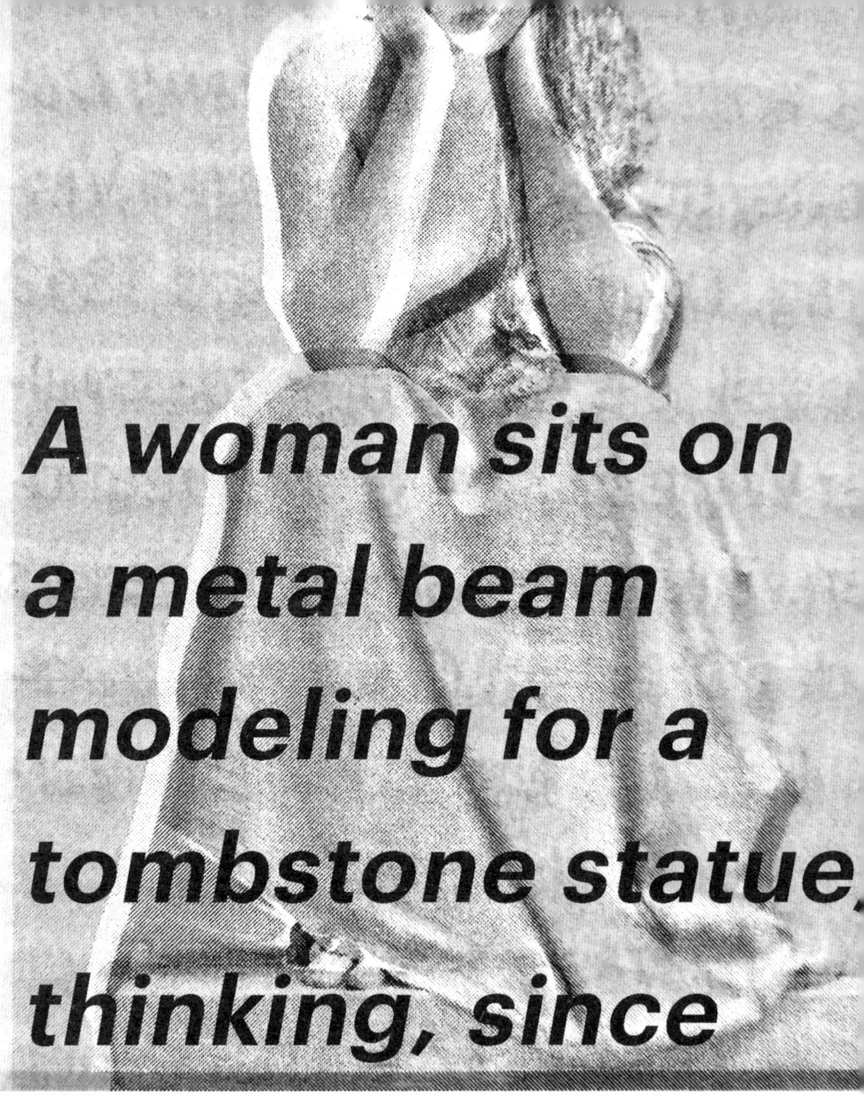

A woman sits on a metal beam modeling for a tombstone statue, thinking, since posing as a model is boring and doesn't pay well

[Figure A puts talcum powder on its whole body, places itself directly in front of the equestrian statue. Figure B moves the projection across the equestrian statue, then moves the light to the performer and back again]

Woman night worker   Today, I will disrupt the work of reproduction. Today, I will be an interruption. At ten am I get back from getting groceries at the train station and make coffee for everyone. On this Sunday morning, I make coffee for the whole house, for all our housemates and their visitors. Today, I will disrupt the work of reproduction. Today I will address the conditions of exploitation. Never mind the Enlightenment and humanism.

Desolation   This is the material speaking!

Woman night worker   Now I cling to his breast. Everywhere the same white plaster. The circle of old men is getting excited, they have not seen anything spectacular in a long time. And seeing is all they can do, since they have been left as busts, their lower bodies cut off – a wise decision for sure.

Offstage voice   He's going to spit on you.

Woman night worker   I'm almost on top, put the mat a little closer in case I miss the handle and slip away, so I would land softly.

Offstage voice   Wait a second; we have a visitor.

Woman night worker   What do you mean by that? Didn't we agree to do this in private?

Offstage voice   Yes, but we have a visitor!

Offstage voice   They took it to heart that the private is now political.

Woman night worker   I'm telling you, I'm loosing my grip, I've been doing this since the 1970s, the private is political and this plaster is incredibly slippery, I'm slipping away, over his shoulder, over his jacket, I'm hurting my chin, and my knees, I leave red traces on the plaster, I'm slipping over the belly of the horse, you push the mat towards me and I fall on it.

Woman night worker   Who will take care of me now that I fell from the horse?

Offstage voice   Fourth passage through history, second version

[Figure A rests on the pedestal of the equestrian statue]

Woman night worker   How does it feel to float around in the dome of the museum? The performance is almost over, everyone is very impressed, you can come back down now.

Offstage voice   There is something on my back. Now it's on my neck, it's soft and ticklish, what could it be?

Comment   Oh, it's someone dusting.

Woman night worker   Why isn't she talking to us?

Offstage voice   She's not allowed to be here, she's invisible.

Comment   She doesn't exist as a role model in the nation-state. Neither in the time when the nation was founded nor now, some felt 100 years later.

Offstage voice [repeats]   'People and goods can now move faster. With the Gotthard base tunnel we bring together people and nations and national economies and build on the pioneering achievements of our ancestors.'

Comment   There is dust trickling down.

Desolation   I'm feeling dusty but not dated! They really did everything to turn my body into a place of reproduction. At the birth of the nation states, they banned me to the domestic sphere, on top of everything.

Woman night worker   Today I am disrupting the work of reproduction. Today I'll do it. Today I'll really do it.

[Figure A brushes off the talcum powder]

Comment   Every sculpture represents a moment frozen in time, even if someone probably posed as a model for many hours. An ideal picture, role models for times long gone.

Woman night worker   Disrupt the work of reproduction.

Comment   The reproduction of gender roles and stereotypes. With one grip, one small disruption – it's no big rupture.

Offstage voice   It only changes the point of view.

Woman night worker   The narrative and its re-telling are interrupted.

Comment   Now the narrative is imploding, the ear falls off,
and the falling narrative is blabbering nonsense.

[Figure A goes around the equestrian statue]

Comment   To feel comfortable, to walk around
                                 To find the books with the wild animals
                                 To stand on the terrace and watch the
                                 gardeners do their gardening
                                 I'm cold
                                 I'm hot
                                 Eat!
                                 I'll pick you up at the hospital
                                 I'll cook some soup for you
                                 I'll bring you a cold washcloth
                                 We'll go dancing together
                                 We'll listen to some music together
                                 We play music together
                                 We live together
                                 We live with many
                                 I'm cleaning up behind me
                                 The guest room is occupied

[Figure B moves the projection across the spaces between the statues]

Offstage voice   Every representation creates exclusions
and invisibilities.

Comment   If no one had dusted here, we would now have
a monument to all those who have preserved the spaces between the
statues for 151 and 118 years, respectively.

Offstage voice   I don't know who these people are, I didn't look
for them and talk to them. But the cleanliness of the room tells me: they

were here! Who restores these statues? So that they can be reproduced, over all these years, in the eyes of all these spectators, as an immaculate picture of the French revolution, of the rising bourgeoisie, of the nation state and its institutions, as a success story.

Comment   I don't know, I didn't talk to them.

[Figure A goes back to Desolation. Puts the pedestal back, doesn't sit down again, but rests its weight on it. Drinks something, eats something]

Offstage voice   Once I was here and it wasn't very orderly. They had taken Spartacus out of the room so that he wouldn't obscure the view of the worker's monument – which is, misleadingly, dedicated to an engineer. I saw how Desolation smirked, I saw how Italy and France turned their heads towards the garden chuckling, I saw how Justitia pulled up the seam of her robe for a moment to see if the rabbits hiding there were doing well. The statues all called each other by their first and family names, they left behind the allegories and Greek goddesses, they put on some clothes or took them off; they powdered themselves, their white was suspicious to them – as if history had been the history of *whites*. 'The Indio woman' pinched Columbus in the calf and laughed at him for all this arrogance, disguised as humanism; the fantastic snakes and sea monsters sneaked out of the books about the exploration of the world that are piled up in the humanist library and got comfortable on a chaise longue.

Comment   Someone is considered a person if they carry a first and a family name, all life long. In private and in public, and it must be the same. For animals, enslaved people, and women, this hasn't been the case until recently.

Woman night worker   Today, I will disrupt the work of reproduction – now that I have had the right to officially participate in national exhibitions as a woman artist for 43 years!

Comment   Does your work day end after your work day,
or does it only then start for real? After you cleaned the statues, will
you then pick up your kids from school and cook a meal, or do you have
another woman from another South that takes care of that for you, so
that you and her and he, outside of the house, somewhere different or
somewhere very different, can go about your paid work?

[Figure B takes a break]

Woman night worker   Examine the working conditions from the
view point of reproductive labour and ask when things have changed for
whom – because someone cleaned, tended to our injuries, shopped for
groceries and cooked them too, listened to what we had to say, slept with
us, gave us emotional stability. If we recount history from the view point
of reproductive labour, work days have always been without beginning
nor end, one kind of work seamlessly followed the next without evenings
nor holidays off, and domestic spaces have always functioned as work
spaces, too – if only in different degrees, depending on people's social
status. The living room served as a space for sewing, instructing, teaching,
and correcting, both for one's own family and for others. We shared the
tasks and then we were isolated.

Offstage voice   Fifth passage through history.

Woman night worker   I'm not going to lie down again. That way, at
least I don't have to get up in the mornings anymore. Even insomnia is
a gendered phenomenon. Today, I will disrupt the work of reproduction.
Today, I will be an interruption.

Comment   I sit there tiredly at the end of a work day,
which could as well be the beginning of one and the same day. There is
still a lot to get done. There is always still a lot to get done.

[Figure B projects the subtitle 'I sit there tiredly at the end of a work day, which
could as well be the beginning of one and the same day. There is still a lot to get done.

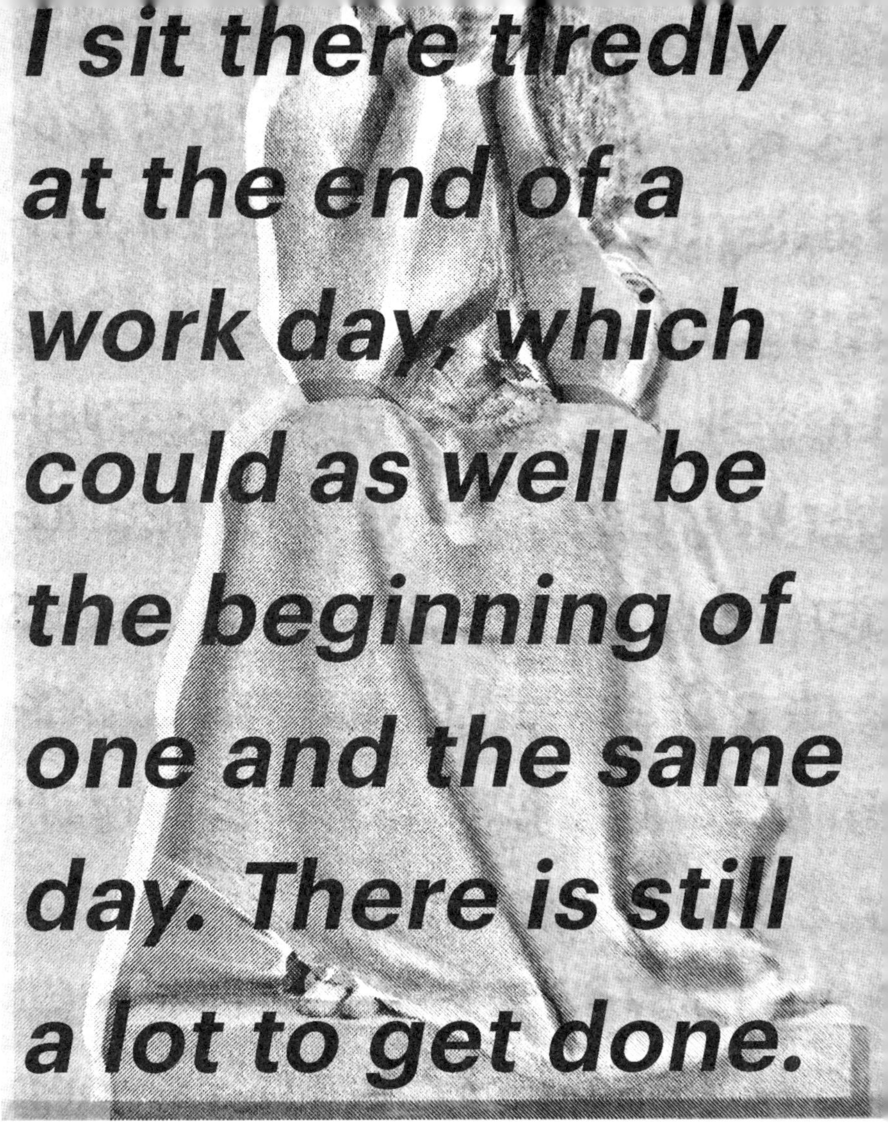

I sit there tiredly
at the end of a
work day, which
could as well be
the beginning of
one and the same
day. There is still
a lot to get done.

There is always
still a lot to get
done.

There is always still a lot to get done.' Figure A takes off its shirt, sits down]

Comment   At what point is someone entitled to not be an allegory, to represent something else, to become a person?

Woman night worker   I like it here, under the pedestal of the equestrian statue; it offers cooling shade and it's nicely polished and clean, too.

Offstage voice   Are you lying comfortably? Does it still hurt?

[Rumbling noises can be heard]

Woman night worker   What were those rumbling noises?

Offstage voice   I think it was a high-speed train passing through the Gotthard base tunnel. The trains passing through there now are so fast. Fast, but not for everyone. They pass fast through the bourgeois values – fast and without stopping!

Comment   Try to imagine the women seasonal workers, at the time of the anti-immigrant 'Schwarzenbach initiative.' In Southern Italy, they've had the right to vote for decades already, and then they come here to this backward place, where women are not allowed to vote, are not allowed to participate in national exhibitions. And now everybody acts as if things had always been the other way around, so they can go about their xenophobia undisturbed. But this is just not true. Try to imagine the nightmares of Justitia. She judges and is just, she has to keep up an appearance so that nobody sees how justice is adjusted from case to case.

Offstage voice   You're getting sidetracked now.

Comment   Maybe we should move things around a little, so that there is no 'main' and no 'side' anymore.

Woman night worker   Long and short emotions. Emotional workers.

So that others can feel good about themselves.

Comment   We have left a trace in the collective memory
that consists of eliminating all traces.

Woman night worker   This too, among others.

Offstage voice   Representational politics is the place where a
narrative insists on its own importance, or, where this insistence can
become a question and a critique of representational politics. Where it
interrupts, implodes; takes away a statue, a statue that suddenly com-
municates from one raw material to the other.

[Figure A gets up, signals to the camera that the performance has ended]

Comment   Wages for Housework is the name of a feminist movement from the 1970s in Italy, whose work is now stored in
an archive in London. To refuse work, the work we do first needs to be
recognized as work. Performance artist Elsa von Freytag-Lothringhover
called it the 'emotional economy' – and I don't think what she meant by
that was historical materialism.

[Reverberations of *Freight Train* by Elizabeth Cotten]

Notes

'Silent colonialism' is the English translation for the Italian definition of 'colonialismo felpato'.

Text References

- A. Brooke, G. Smith, R. Farkas (eds.), *Re-Materialising Feminism*, Arcadia Missa, London 2014
- Silvia Federici, *Wages Against Housework*, Power of Women Collective and Falling Wall Press, Bristol 1975
- Gosteli–Stiftung Archive, Bern 1973
- E-mail lists about the refugee camp in Como, Summer 2016
- Swiss Federal Railways SBB, blog about the opening of the Gotthard Base Tunnel, 2015-2016
- Ceremonial speech at the inauguration of the Gotthard Base Tunnel, June 2016
- Swiss art guide 'Swiss Kunstführer GSK', Museo Vincenzo Vela, Ligornetto 2003
- Booklets, Museo Vincenzo Vela, Ligornetto 2016

Sound references

- *Who am I?* by The Fates, in 'Furia', LP 1985
- *Freight Train* by Elizabeth Cotten, in 'Folksongs and Instrumentals With Guitar', LP 1958

Sounds Like Metal – I Am the Wall
Where Will You Be Main Frequencies

The audio-based performance follows several trains of thoughts on shared subject positions, and a group of gendered and futuristic digital voice pre-sets on their search for colonial legacies in speech. Their journey is unsuccessful; the Royal Museum for Central Africa in Tervuren, outside of Brussels, is under reconstruction. The search drifts, and the spaces of the museum and the storage where the performance takes place overlap. Ghosting voices in a former storage space for colonial goods.

Speakers, a subwoofer, spotlights and signs are placed on either side of the wall dividing the space. Sounds like metal, sound joined rooms, alternating repetitions and loops. The voice of the recorded and the live spoken sequences is the same, modulated in pitch, tone and spatiality by different recording conditions, digital pre-set, channels and a subwoofer.

Short descriptions of the performer's movements appear on the side. The audience sits or moves along – listening as positioning in space.

Seated besides subwoofer. Starting externalised voice tracks

This is who is here today
I am a fiction

I am a fiction
I am a fiction

The I today
I am a fiction

I am a fiction   *The I today*
I am a fiction

The I today
I am a fiction

[live] It begins without me

Reinforcing the I
Destabilising the I
Eating the I
Unlearning the I

Introducing the voices
And their characters at play

[live] The bright and the classical, followed by the compressed and the dance vocal. An edge, a fuzz, a narration or a natural vocal. A stammered, a telephone, a tracking, a tube, a tuned, a vintage, a warm vocal. Different experimental vocals. Deeper, delay, helium, megaphone, monster, robot vocal. Crushed, distorted, electrified, filtered, flanged, phased, ringshifted, time machine.

Walking towards
the spread public

You are in
A place with four rooms
And shared spaces

Speaking in
relation to visible
and invisible walls

[live] How did you come to this place? By boat or by foot? And under which name? Were you profiled by skin colour to enter? Did someone ask you about your sex, your sexuality, your income, your bank account? Were you judged by the way you speak? Were there other invisible lines?

You can hear steps
Walking towards the wall
That divides the space

[Steps can be heard on the other side of the wall]

The Own and The Other enter the room

[Steps on this side of the wall, approaching]

You can hear steps finding
Their position in space

[Steps, very close]

Have you found a place to stand?

You are standing on: my cultural preset
– and I am sitting on yours

[Subwoofer plays alone]

Sitting down on
the subwoofer and
leveling it up

[live] Social spaces applied to sound wave patterns.
Signal chains, adding to the tone of the voices in
play. Wave patterns that we hear as standardised,
normalised voices. Coding and decoding tones
and intonations. Positioned for or against, within
or with a critical distance. The observer's distance.
The one that records, describes, collects, comments,
judges, brings home.

This is who is here today –
The I today,
        I am a fiction

        The I today
        I am a fiction

            I am a fiction

I am a fiction

Reinforcing the I
destabilizing the I
eating the I
unlearning the I.

Standing up,
stoping in front
of the wall

The Own and the Other enter the room

[live] Speaking in relation to: That wall. *White*,
middle-class, heteronormative patriarchy, it's geni-
uses, cultures, and institutions. The construction
of a history of winners, of names and authorships,
of singular figures, in the logic of bloodlines and
names. This is the wall that I am speaking against,
the social wall that I want to shift. Before, as and
while I will turn around. It's an invisible wall. It's
the wall of exclusion.

Turning around
Turning around

A field without center
Protagonists, side figures, fists

In the door frame,
turning one of the
spots. The ray of
light gets divided
by the wall

[live] The wall becomes a component that not only
marks a separation, but is also a compositional
element; one that joins rooms through sound, by
marking a here and there. The partition becomes
a joyful element, a situation for listening through
movements in space.

Turning around.

   A field without centre,

   protagonists, side figures,

   fists

[Subwoofer alone]

I am the wall –
Where will you be
Main frequencies

[live] Not listening, listening. A proposal for a
non-normative listening literacy.

   History is closed today

   History is being renovated

   It begins without me

[Three metallic knocks, marking the beginning of a song]

The metal I find
I find it in the streets

      Reverb

      Reverse

         The bullet cuts the air backwards

         Your arm hits the ground

                                                      Dropping a bunch
                                                      of metallic objects
                                                      such as keys

               Footsteps on

The high tones down,
Only the sub is playing
Recalling, the sound of metal

Low,
Laying down on the ground,
The memory passes above you

The future according to metal
Was always: faster

Contemporary warfare,
The soft skills of ignorance

The future according to metal
is still endlessly faster

[Three metallic knocks, marking the beginning of a song]

Sitting down in
the back side of
the space

Let's go and see how all of this is stored and displayed
at the local museum of colonial self-representation

[Reverbs, several times]

[live] The voices and their adjectives in play:
The bright and the classical vocal, light and clear
and luminous, in a tiny tram on the way to the
colonial museum. The compressed and the dance
vocal: bleached hair, light skin, grey nails, passing
woods and parks. The edge and the fuzz vocal: feel
entitled to join. The narration and the natural vocal:

guarding the palm trees of Western ideals. The
stammered and the telephone vocal: wish to abandon
distant relationships. The tube and the tuned,
the vintage vocal: miss daylight, get confused.
The warm vocal: longs for someone to be close to.
The experimental vocals, in front of closed doors
and a construction site.

It's me! Your colonial legacies in speech

We don't need
Main frequencies

> *It's over now*
> *Your white fading time*

> *It's over now*
> *your equalising*

[live] 'Equality is what is offered as legal rights to
colonised people. And what is imposed on them
is culture. Culture is the principle through which
those with hegemonic power continue to control
those without.'

They lower their tones

Adding a more authoritarian signal

Deep and delayed

> *Let's go and see how all of this is stored*
> *and displayed – at the local museum*
> *of colonial self representation*

[Reverbs, several times]

History is closed today
History is being renovated

Find your colonial legacies in speech
Somewhere else
Find your colonial legacies in recording devices
Somewhere else – online

[Subwoofer alone]

The journey is an internal one
The museum is under reconstruction

[Three metallic knocks, marking the beginning of a song]

Walking around

[live] The journey is an internal one. The space is this one here. Storage space, divided or composed by walls. Discharged cargo, voice tones, and sound wave patterns.

> *I am the cargo*
> *The ghost of those*
> *The ghost of me*
> *The ghost inside*

[live] Who is here today and how will you read or change my voice. Breaks, cuts. Breaking with or within a linear history of exclusion. The tone of a surface, the taste of listening, the patterns of recognition.

> *The waves of privilege*
>
> *Your helium filter is calming me down*
>
> *Find your colonial legacies in recording devices*
> *somewhere else – inside*

[live] What is your voice tone wearing today? Something neutral? Or something that makes noise, that makes the body and its movements audible? Never just: straight. Never just: gay. Never just: feminist. Never just: universal keyword. Never just: hegemonic sound.

Sitting on the subwoofer

[live] What is your position in space? The room as resonance and response at the same time. Speaking in relation to: reverb maybe. Listening in relation to: the conglomerate of word patterns, rhythms, intonations, intentions and their extensions. Speaking in relation to: the bodies in this room that break the sound wave, depending on their position in space towards what I say.

[Subwoofer alone]

[live] Listening to: spaces that reverberate. That resonate. That extend the bodies and voices crossing. An invisible archive of spoken history, of pasts and passings. Sound joined rooms. Imaginary friends and futures. Active and passive vocabulary. The crossroads of our wording. Our finding and inventing of words. The materials we collaborate with. The sounds that realise the listening practices that

we practice every day. The sentences that we hand over in daily conversations. Forms of shared thinking and authorships. Modulating the space carefully.

Back to the
first room

[Three metallic knocks, marking the beginning of a song]

She enters the room from the left side
Assigned the markers of invisibility

Dressed as
Dressed as herself without self
– she says

Who can I possibly be in these streets between my home and my studio, my work and my workplace?

Who can I possibly be, when being listened to by you?

You say the nation state
I say domestication

You say the abandonment of that state

I said
Always related to
Never just masculine, never just white
Never just middle-class genius

[live] The self, the achievement of a self, is a phantasy
of the West from the 19th century: power, domestication, gender assignements, ownerships – capitalist
principles inside and outside private space. As
legitimations for racialised and gendered power
relationships. The binary space does not allow for
any inbetweens or beyonds.

                  How to be queer

                  in a binary space.

A bullet cuts the air
The sound is hissing
I could not say that I heard it exactly

The way I memorise it now

But it was very close to my ear
I couldn't say I was there
But it was very close to my ear

A tiny voice, a leaden voice
In a tiny tram on their search
For colonial legacies in speech.

– Still on our way to the local museum,
A construction site, the walls
The facades of colonial binds.

Reinforcing the I
Destabilising the I
Eating the I
Unlearning the I

What is your position in space?

Sitting on the
subwoofer

[live] Your masculinity reverberates, self-authorising frequencies assigned. The low voice is assigned to a canon of singular figures, on top of the social scale. In Europe, at least, most often a marker beyond the world of properties, dependencies, and objects.
The object is one that breaks the waves, that is placed in space, that makes a space reverberant or dry.
It might be a plant, or a speaker, a wallpaper, or another element. A body for example.

Invisibility

The binary space does not allow
For any inbetweens

[live] To intervene into reproduction. Entangling a voice that does not fit the standardised combination of attributes and adjectives; of voice, of hair, of physical constitution, of health, of care, of housing, of reproductive labour, of authorship and authority.

You are in
A space with four rooms
And shared space

Voices break or don't – socially

Your voice is breaking
In the first room
Of that place

Breaking into
Sound waves of joy

> *The second room hosts the break*
> *With stabilised narration*

> *It is what you say in a third room*
> *That is connected to this second room*
> *Via small holes*
> *Through them*
> *One can hand or stick*
> *Or listen closely*

> *What you say stays unclear*
> *It's an undecided sexuality that speaks*

In the morning I'm a bird
Slowly towards noon
My voice lowers

> *I negotiate*
> *After sun set*
> *I go out*

Cruising in the parks
And in other people's phantasies
Other people's phantasies
Shared ones, tinny and rattingly shared
Fear and excitement at the same time

One night that I remember very well –

Getting up

[live] The tinny voice is one that misses lower frequencies. It misses what is assigned to masculine authority. It's one that makes us afraid. Are we afraid of missing lower frequencies? We connect its excitement to hysterics and therefore write it out of history. A history of winners, of top shots, of hits and strikes, of war and warlords, of technology developped for these wars.

The tinny voice seems to remind us
Of our own disabilities, uncompletednesses.

[live] They seem to remind us on the connection of voice break and warfare, between masculinity and the construction of gender binaries and genderunequalities, as Pınar Selek writes. Shaped by war, by warfare.

[Metallic knock]

Seventy years of peace,
the restaurant owner of Asmara says,
on his country's 25th independence day

[Metallic knock]

> *The Own and the Other*
> > *The Own and the Other*
> *Get involved in shootings around that time*

How do you remember those days? And now?

> *She gets up and says*

> *With a calm*
> *A subtitling*
> *A documentary voice*

[live] A technical, technological scale that co-
designs the vocabulary through which we hear
and communicate. As it has established itself
through industrial standartisation, electrification,
digitalisation, quantification, normalization of
wandering magnet fields. Transmitted, sent and
received, modulated by interpretation. A technical
vocabulary to describe qualities of speaking and the
gendered values connected to them.

> *She gets up*
> *She walks out*

> *With a trembling*
> *A shimmering*
> *Rainbowish tone*

I forgot a part of myself out there
I don't know if I can go get it now

Still on our way to the colonial museum
A wall, the facades of colonial binds

They will not arrive today

Maybe you forgot about your Self. Partly at least.
Until you come across the place where it took place.
The place, it's smell, it's sound, and texture will
remind you.

[Three metallic knocks, marking the beginning of a song]

Going to where   *The own and the other got lost by the way*
the key chain was   *– in a tiny tram way on their search*
dropped on the   *For colonial legacies in speech*
floor, picking it up   *In an affirmative self-sabotage*
                         An anthropophagic festivity

They will not arrive today

They are still on their way

I am the ghost of what can not be heard

In Western tones and binary scales

I interrupt and circulate

I misunderstand and disconnotate
For fundamental change

It begins witout me

[live] I remember a bullet crossing the air. The tinny
voice was not around anymore after that, she says,
and eats up the microphone that was placed in front
of her head in order to measure, to prevent, to bring
home.

[One hears a lavalier microphone getting swallowed]

I am a fiction
– the I today

       The I today
       I am a fiction

              I am a fiction

I am a fiction

Me who has dissolved
Me who has disappeared
Me who is being recodified

Me who is imagined,

descentralised,

shared, always entagled

and related.

[live] Your adjectives are simple, simply pro-
grammed sound waves, common sense. Gender
categories as they were established through and by
processes of colonisation. Recording technologies,
to control, to conserve.

The passage can be everyhwhere, he says

70 years of peace, 70 years of deconstructing patriarchy

[Playing *Chaupele Mpenzi*]

The Walls *is an anti-colonial play by Jean Genet. Playing with stereotypical figures, 96 six of them – each actor plays several. In French, there are mobile paravents. They become 'screens' in English and in German: walls.*

Leaving the storage space, the back yard, the city, until the wireless microphone loses contact

I am the Wall *is a poem by Pat Parker. Over-affirming stereotyped attributes of deviant sexuality as figures of resistance.*

Text references

- Jean Genet, *Les Paravents*, L'Arbalète, Décines 1961
- Sylvia Wynter, *On Being Human as Praxis*, Duke University Press, Durham 2015
- Pınar Selek, *Zum Mann gehätschelt. Zum Mann gedrillt. Männliche Identitäten*, Orlanda Verlag, Berlin 2010
- Carla Lonzi, *Let's spit on Hegel*, 1974. 'Equality is what is offered to colonized people and what is imposed on them as culture. Culture is the principle through which those with hegemonic power continue to control those without'

Sound references

- *I am the Wall* by Pat Parker, in 'Where Would I Be Without You', LP 1976
- *Nali kisafiri* by Coast Social Orchestra and *Chaupele Mpenzi* by Dar-Es Salaam Swingers, Ally K. Sykes, in 'Colonial Dance Bands. 1950–1952', CD 2008. Found in 2010 at the Central Africa Museum in Tervuren

Places involved

- The Central Africa Museum, Tervuren 2010/2017
- Montgomery metro/tram station, Brussels 2017
- Tram from Montgomery to Tervuren, 2010/2017
- Quai des charbonnages 30-34, Molenbeek Brussels, 2016/2017

The text describes a journey to a small village in the countryside, near by the German border. A highway separates the village from a natural resort and a former garbage depot, where now a shipping container sits. The performance is written from the perspective of a visitor, one who grew up here. Reading landscape design along memories and actualities as places of protection and exposition, describing racism and processes of othering. The text was written after a row of petitions for a referendum that tightened federal and communal laws on asylum and migration policies. The performance begins with sequences of movements.

[Projection on, stepping into the image, showing a sequence of movements]

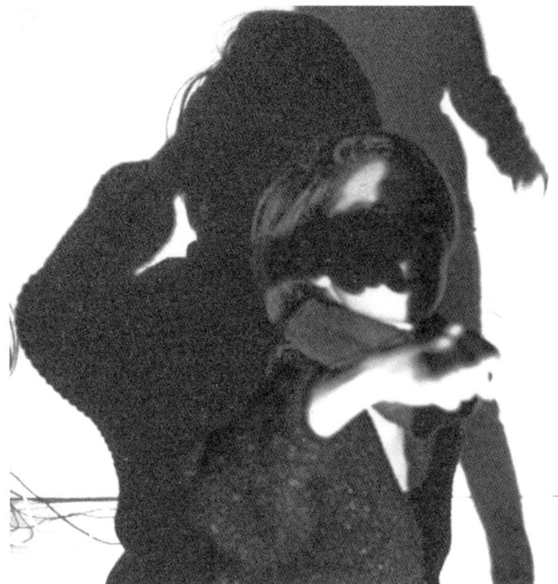

I am interested in how this movement becomes this movement, how one movement becomes another.

A friend recently said: an urgency is not an emergency. What if a situation is both?

I take a train from the main station. The train is stuffed with commuters ending their working day. The train stops every other minute at another station. Crossing the suburbs, passing the airport, passing first one farm then another. I leave the train and I take a yellow post-bus. The bus stops in every village. In every hamlet. At each stop two or three passengers leave the bus. The bus now crosses a nature reserve, famous for its endangered birds. The children of this region learn how to recognize their voices. It was in my first year at primary school when I learned how to carry frogs across these streets that cross their land, that cross the nature reserve. The street on which the bus is driving now, separating their spawning ground from the swamp where they pass most of their time.

The birds would come back to the nature reserve during summer time. On the surrounding farms, seasonal workers from eastern Europe would join for the harvests of the strawberries and the corn.

The first person who was placed in the village as an asylum seeker by cantonal authorities was a man from the former Yugoslavia who had fled the war. One refugee. That was already enough. There was a general fear in the village that he would bring his family too, assumed to be traumatized and therefore violent people. And so he did. They were given an old run-down farmer's house close to the bus stop in a small street towards the nature reserve.

The bus leaves the highway and the nature reserve behind, we arrive. The bus stops at the bus stop that used to be my bus stop. I cross the main road and head towards the end of the town, towards the nature reserve.

The village's borders are defined by the nature reserve surrounding it. Because of the nature reserve it will not grow bigger. It is the highway that marks the end of the village and the beginning of the nature reserve.

There is a small bridge for pedestrians that crosses the highway. At the foot of the bridge on the other side there is an almost hidden ground for the caretakers to bring old leaves and garbage there – everything that doesn't belong. A very practical place: the garbage removal can stop directly, without leaving the highway almost. But it is also a dangerous spot – cars and gravel trucks are passing here at full speed. A noisy spot, not actually the entrance to the heavenly place – what the nature reserve still is in my memory.

It was a place where you could hide the village – its phobias and social control. In the nature reserve there were no billboards announcing the one and only party represented in the local council of the town. Advertising strong slogans such as: 'Foreigners out of here!' In the nature reserve there were no flags that would remind you in which country you were, just in case you had forgotten during your daily walk to the village store.

The design of the town makes clear that there are strictly defined zones where humans can build and live – which also include fields and woods for cultivating. And a zone for nature, the nature reserve, where protected animals and plants would live. If both parties wouldn't bother each other, everything was in order, everything was fine.

I crossed the bridge that crosses the highway, that leads from the village to the zone of nature and savage animals. At the foot of the bridge, a very noisy and dangerous spot, a square where the garbage car used to stop. I find an old container that is placed where old leaves and garbage were deposited all the years before – I just went back to check my memory. The kind of shipping container that we know from construction sites. The ones that are built to a globally standardized size.

A container that can be put on a lorry, on a train, on a boat, that can be shipped from here to everywhere. A container that marks a temporary space, a space that will be moved one day, a space that is not a space where one can stay.

When I discovered the containers, placed on the temporary garbage place, it was the first time that I saw people waiting for asylum again on the village's ground. I was shocked about the clear language that the village's officials had found for their xenophobia. A place so clearly marking an outsider space, a temporary space, one of the few spots out of the village's sight. Nature's site, the site for birds and frogs and plants.

Like most villages and towns in the region, this village also refused to offer places to asylum seekers this time but was obliged by the canton to do so however. The village's politicians found their defiant answer – on the side of the road.

Racism begins by dividing the world into binaries, into protected zones and shooting zones, into natural places and civilized spheres, into privilege and surrender. These zones can be marked and detached, by streets and houses and trees. They are marked by squares and zones of noises and smells. The smell of a grassland and the smell of a garbage place. You will remember the smell, even if the garbage is not there anymore. Some people will remember this smell. Others will not. Places are coded.

––––––––

Cutback: First we took the space and then we took the space. How can you take something that belongs to you anyway. We took the space and we lived the space and we left the space. How can you leave something that does not exist anymore.

When she was my age she left society. She left to leave.

Notes

Two years after this text was written, the containers were gone. I rediscovered the containers beside my workplace at the art university, beside my studio in the outskirts of Zurich, on the air field of Tempelhof in Berlin. Always in abandoned transition spaces, camps, that would make clear: you didn't come here to stay. When the containers had been moved away, the refugeed were accommodated at the former pub of the town. I was told about a new mayor and that the political pressure from the canton had become too high.

Saisonarbeiter or *Saisonier*, translated in English as 'Seasonal worker' (guest worker), was the name given to workers hired from abroad for nine months maximum per year under the Saisonnierstatut from 1934. Workers with such a contract were not allowed to bring their families along, and were usually underpaid and without social insurances.

[Sound bit]

Welcome to the newsreel of Week 29/2014 on barış fm. Live from the Hal Binası in Sinop on the occasion of Sinopale. My name is Aslı.

The first question we are concerned with in this week's newsreel:

Did you ever consider murdering your husband? If so: how would you do it? Would you poison his food, choke him in his sleep, run him over with a car, lock him up in the cellar and let him die of hunger? Or quite simply shoot him with a handgun – of the sort that are on sale in common shops on the main street?

Here are some voices on this from Sinop:

I would simply get a divorce. But I could also imagine dropping him off at my autoritarian father's mountain shelter, accessible by helicopter only.

This is the advice of a collaborator of Sinopale, presupposing a mountain shelter on the one hand. Finding an authoritarian father in Central Europe on the other hand, is no problem. Her friend agrees:

'You should ask this question to the women quartered in the prison of Sinop. We should strengthen international women's solidarity in a way that such acts of despair are no longer needed. The female body seen from an other perspective than from its external and internal constraints. Nobody kills another for fun. But when a person becomes the prison of another, prevents them from developing their talents and needs, it seems appropriate to me to tear down these prison walls that block the view onto the sea.'

[Sound bit]

You know, it occurs to me that in English women who survive their husbands are called husband killers.

[Sound bit]

In the former post building of Sinop a door was found this week that is impossible to reach. No stairs lead to this door, which was ostensibly placed in the upper right corner of the room by mistake when the building was erected, instead of providing a passage to the terrace. As a consequence a rumor spread, claiming that through this door, it is possible to find the figures that have gone missing.

[Sound bit]

This week the two writers Ella Maillart and Annemarie Schwarzenbach visited our studio on their Afghan Journey. As they drop by in Sinop, the two women are fleeing from the war. They are often mistaken for German spies and complain about the devastation caused by technical progress also in the young Turkey. In *All the Roads are Open*, writes Annemarie Schwarzenbach in 1939 about her trip:

'For the present we glide through the Bosporus on the white, silently tamping steamer Ankara, and the waterway between green, sloping banks is so lovely that one is hard-pressed to be reminded of the meaning of this name, of an entirely different kind, grave in the great game for war and peace. And the Black Sea, despite the sometimes asiatically barren hills, is fed by the air and light, color and gaiety of the Mediterranean. The steamer anchors off small harbours, off Inebolu and Sinope, off

Samsoun and Girson; each time an entire fleet of heavy fishing boats takes to the sea to welcome us. The lads stem their feet against the front plank and row as if for their life; load carriers, sellers of cherries and bread climb onboard; in a few minutes the forward deck of the elegant steamer is turned into a market place, and our Ford car serves to stack merchandise and as a shop stall; the merchant sits on the footboard with his round, flat breads; on the baggage rack a cheerful boy pitches pink-color ice-cream.'

Yes it is the same boat! that we see on the picture as the one that is exhibited in front of Sinop fortress prison. That I can see very well on the picture of the two women's journey from 1938 that you are showing me. Says one of the guards of Sinop prison museum.

With Ella Maillart 'the open roads' become *The Cruel Way*, which she publishes only after WWI, and after Annemarie's death:

'We also anchored for a few hours off the harbours – Inebolu, Sinope, Samsoun, Girasun. Men climbing their way up the hull along hanging lines; pushing through the noisy crowds of the maindeck, offering cherries and blackberries, bread, baskets, ribbons and flowers. Our Ford becoming the baker's counter: he, standing on the running-board with his loaves displayed on the hood.'

[Sound bit]

While building up Sinopale 5 a strange door was discovered. Artists participating now deliberate on that.

The tourism minister congratulates us for reactivating abandoned buildings in the city center and thanks us for rising the value of these buildings deriving from this. The community on the other side are hoping that these buildings become accessible again for the inhabitants of Sinop and escape to disappear as private property and real-estate speculation – despite their valorization.

[Sound bit]

Deniz Süz sends us this letter. She is studying quantum physics in Istanbul and spends the summer months in Sinop at her relatives place on the seaside. Thereby, something strange happened to her, which as a physicist she thinks must have to do with nuclear energy.

'Today I woke up and she was no longer there. Like every morning I turned around to cuddle up to her for some more minutes. Even before I had turned around all the way I knew that this morning the other side of the bed would be cool and empty towards the otherwise so soft movements of the waves. Even so, I am startled as I stretch out my arm. She is no longer there: her white body that she never lays under the blazing sun is no longer there.

Her full body, unspoiled from swimming in the sea, with the mask-like face with fair make-up above, whose light shimmer she does not relinquish even in her sleep, is no longer there. If she had gotten up to leave I would have heard her. I did not hear her get up, though, and in this moment of waking I ask myself whether she has ever lain there, all these balmy nights next to me. A pain pulls on my breast, seemingly already understanding everything that I cannot know yet. She is gone. No longer here.

I sit up and glance over the untouched bed sheet to the sea. No dent, no wrinkle hints at this, that last night Jîn, as ever wonderful, slightly disgruntled, was still lying next to me from head to toes. The roll of the waves that always makes me feel so pleased, now suddenly seems aggressive, unyielding, demanding. I lean forward to close the window. And I see, under the window in the shade of the morning sun, a woman posing in an improvised photo studio from bygone times.

I found her picture in an old album at the flea market, searching for texts by the travel writer Annemarie Schwarzenbach. This is why in my narration, her story is directly connected to Annemarie's. The caption under the picture reads: "Her face is round and white, her hands laid out on a stand."

With her back upright, she watches the sea through the loose leaves. I want to grasp at her. The quiet present of the image soothes my pain over the absent, even this morning. The dazzling dots of her dress glisten in the sun, which through the swaying leaves plays with her silhouette. Only now I slowly lift up my head, there, where the absent becomes the picture of an Ottoman princess. I do not want to understand, even now. It is not proven yet that it is nuclear power that makes the characters merge or disappear from the stories.'

We wish Deniz good luck with her search. We would like to point out that the activities against the construction of the nuclear plant are going on also during the summer.

[Sound bit]

Following the Afghan Journey two young women set out from an inn in Monte Carlo to a journey to Kirkuk. Not only for the delicate sounds of the names, but also. The names are linked in the same sense as are A and Ânif, Anifen and Bali, Bali and Brassens on the spine of the Meydan Larousse encyclopedia.

[Sound bit]

A great advantage the Turkish language could have in renegotiating gender roles is the personal pronoun 'o', as artist Aylin Tekiner explains:

Speaking a lot of English with the artists from abroad I realize once more, why I often mix up he, she, it: because in Turkish we only use the personal pronoun 'o' for all genders and also for things.

This is not to say that the personal pronoun 'o' is about making all equal. 'o' can name an infinite number of possibilities of gender roles: it makes no clear divide between men and women, between humans and things and opens a variety of perspectives on how gender roles can be negotiated in the use of language and at every level of grammar and language structure. The sociologist and feminist Pınar Selek was unfortunately not reachable on the phone on her exile in France to comment.

[Sound bit]

In the middle of the week we have been informed about the passing away of patriarchy. In the mean time the two travel writers Annemarie Schwarzenbach and Ella Maillart are traversing the Black Sea in the direction of Trabzon on the wooden boat of the prison museum, undertaking their Afghan Journey.

[Sound bit]

Some comments on the foreground, and some on the background. And some on the coulisse: In the background a canvas. A sailcloth. The silhouette of a medium size Amazon stands out from it. She is dressed, and so it is difficult to say clearly whether she is an Amazon, whether and for what reasons her right breast has been amputated.

In memory it is often the case that characters coalesce with the background, merge with it and become different beings from what they were in their time.

This is a small reference to the film *Jîn* by Reha Erdem and the 19th Festival on Wheels Sinop about which we have reported earlier.

[Sound bit]

This reminds me of Sabahattin Ali, that permanent resident of the prison museum in the Fortress Prison Sinop, with mirror cabinet and eiderdown quilt.

Look at the words of Sabahattin Ali. Do you know what they stand for, besides what you see literally and with the help of your own cultural metaphors. How and where these poems have come into existence, how they became known, how they turned from poem to song lyrics. Why they made this career. How their translation came about, their journey through the most varied languages of the world. *Aldırma Gönül* for instance, or the Madonna in Fur.

The Madonna, this Christian mother figure. That in Catholicism compulsively and indiscriminately relegates women to their role as self-sacrificing and caring, as crying mothers.

You see these words on white paper in a book. The foreground and background in this case are contained in the text. The sheet of paper as a neutral carrier, a norm we have learned to assume to be invisible. In the case of literature, foreground and background begins to interest us in the context of site-specific writing. What could site-specific writing be?

[Sound bit]

On their stop in Sinop two young travelers told us about a white whale they have seen at the estuary of the Black Sea. Fishermen from Sinop also told us about it. We found a report to that effect from 1982.

A white whale is not the same as a white elephant. A white whale stands for luck. A white elephant however stands for collective memory that every individual carries with them in their unconscious, that keeps reappearing, possibly precisely when one believes to have finally forgotten it.

The news of the white whale triggered long discussions in our editorial team, for at the same time various newspapers report that the recently affirmed right to be forgotten in the Internet clashes with the freedom of the press. This right to be forgotten cannot be compared, of course, to links being barred for reasons of censorship, or servers being confiscated. Or to being impossible-to-find because the body to the words has disappeared.

[Sound bit]

We ask ourselves whether the fact that Sinop this year again is considered the happiest city in Turkey, as our National Office for Statistics let us know, is still related to the white whale.

A report on the daily progress in developing a quantum computer and the hopes lying in it for infinitely fast and concurrent access to archives, based not on a 'yes' or a 'no' but on concurrency, will be the object of an in-depth broadcast next week in which Deniz Süz will also participate. We will deal with the question of whether this concurrency of quantum physics can be compared to the concurrency that allows the use of historical present tense.

[Sound bit]

Some remarks on the difference between fiction and science fiction: science fiction is a genre of literature that has grown with the belief in technical progress. The shifting of martial and imperialistic efforts to space characterizes science fiction in most cases.

Fiction on the other hand does not relate primarily to science. It deals with inter-human relations, current social conditions, characters, places, the invisible. It is thus possible to locate both the future and the past in a historical present and thereby undermine, using grammatical means familiar to us all, the power of linear thinking, storytelling and historicizing.

[Sound bit]

This week we also got news from the World Tuning Organization. It makes a call to the population of Sinop to record the voices of the incoming refugees from Syria. There will be a listening station in the newly renovated library, where these voices can be retrieved from a server. Sinop is to become a center for oral history and collect such recordings from the entire region.

[Sound bit]

Imagine there is something there, on Twitter for instance, and you cannot read it. Not because you cannot read or do not understand the language but because what is written there has been made invisible. The message is still there but you cannot see it. You then need contact to someone who can see it; in another country it might work.

On this occasion we read out the profile of the wanted person, with the request that she won't be confused with Ella Maillart, Jîn or the neighbor who is already well known: Red-haired hacker – likes to wear a cloth in front of her face.

Should you know anything about her whereabouts, please send any clues to barış fm.

There is a listener calling, who would like to comment:

The woman on this photo is a princess from the Ottoman Empire times. You can see this on the way she wears her make up and her clothing, the way she poses for the picture. Yes it's very clear.

Says the same man that has also identified the boat in front of the prison as the one on which Annemarie Schwarzenbach and Ella Maillard crossed the Black Sea with their Ford.

We have reached the end of our broadcast. Many thanks for listening, and join us next week again in Sinop. For the translation I thank Nilüfer Sülüner, Alain Kessi and Frank Hagen, barış fm and the team of Sinopale 5. In the studio at the microphones, Aslı says goodbye.

[Sound bit]

Notes

In June 1939, Annemarie Schwarzenbach and fellow writer Ella Maillart set out from Geneva in a Ford, heading to Afghanistan. Traveling on Afghanistan's Northern Road, they fled the storm brewing in Europe to seek a place untouched by what they considered to be the Western neuroses.
Some of the women imprisoned in Sinop's women prison are accused of murdering their husbands. In most cases the women acted out of self-defense.
Shortly before Sinopale 5 the Turkish Government decided to build the first nuclear plant in Turkey only a few kilometers away from Sinop, despite massive protests and mobilizations against it from the local communities.
The cell of Sabahattin Ali has been retrospectively displayed and furnished in the museum of the Sinop Tarihi Cezaevi (Sinop fortress prison).

Text references

– Songül Ketenci, Women's Rights Organisation Sinop
– Annemarie Schwarzenbach, *All the Roads are Open. The Afghan Journey*, University of Chicago Press, Chicago 2000
– Ella Maillart, *The Cruel Way. Switzerland to Afghanistan in a Ford, 1939*, University of Chicago Press, Chicago 2013
– Meydan Larousse is the largest encyclopedia published in Turkish. As found in the hotel's living room
– Pınar Selek, *Zum Mann gehätschelt. Zum Mann gedrillt. Männliche Identitäten*, Orlanda Verlag, Berlin 2010
– *Weisser Wal im Schwarzen Meer*, in 'NZZ', 19 February 1992
– Unknown sources

Protagonists of this performance are placeholder figures, wildcard symbols and silhouettes. An image circulates, printed on cotton fabric to be exported to customers in the Ottoman empire in the same year when a 'strike led by women and children' took place in the same factory. The women, though, appear only as statistical numbers in documents around that first strike in the early-industrialised valley of Glarus, Switzerland. The strike followed the mounting of a bell that introduced a fixed beginning of the working day. Improvements in working conditions and factory laws followed only years later.

A glass pane and a projector are used to amplify the outline of different paper signs. A contact microphone feeds back the slight touch of the papers being placed on the glass.

You just entered the space and are still looking for a place. You have already been here for a while. You are still on your way. Maybe you won't make it today.

[Testing microphone]

[Stepping in from the side room]

[Standing behind the glass table]

This is where I work.

And here is who I work with:

[Taking a photo of women workers in a textile printing factory out of the trousers pockets, passing it around]

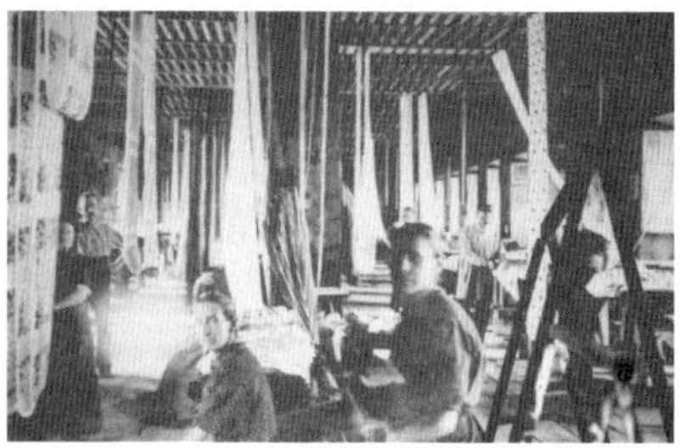

[Taking individualised silhouettes out of the publication, placing them on the glass]

a looks towards b, whilst c and d –

[Taking four wild card symbols '#,!,~,$'out of the publication; placing them on the glass]

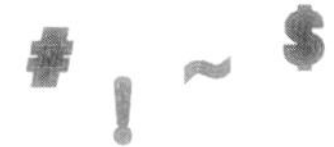

Should I pitch your voice slightly?
a and b stand against the light

Is this where the fabric of the sketch is? The museum is still over-worked. I am told that my request and all the other requests about the collection endanger the development of the next special exhibition. All the while the image found emerges beneath my hands – my image of you and your image of me 'an image from the 19th century that still resonates' emerges beneath my hands, 18 hours a day, also in the winter.

[Holding up the sketch 'A Fabric in Turkey Red with a Fareastern Pattern']
[Passing around the sketch]

c and d stand a bit off-set

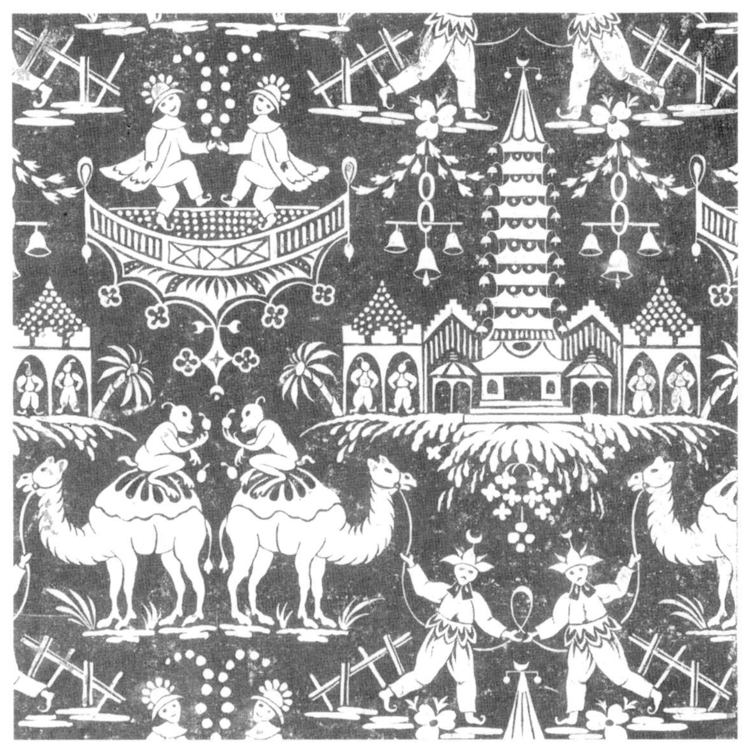

[Shifting slightly the position of the symbols '#, !, ~, $' on the glass]

Is there a connection between printing template, image motif, the workers' strike and emigration, apart from a concurrence of industrial production measures, mass production and mass emigration?

Wild cards – placeholders that can stand in for other figures depending on search criteria and language politics.

[Placing asterisk and more wild cards '*, ", [,], §, ƒ, ∞' on the glass]

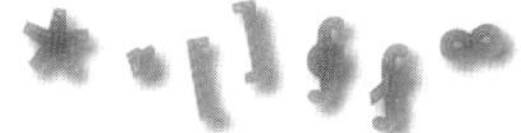

A placeholder figure, suggesting possibility.
– c towards d: Again it is about the search for a figure

It's diffuse –

someone has been producing this – eighty percent women and children as the statistics say – without leaving a fingerprint.

I ask about you
Everywhere where I wish you would be
I am asking about you
I flip books open and close them again
Everywhere that I guess you may be –
I leave them on my writing table
Until the lending period runs out

b reaches for a free sign

[Placing pictures of silhouettes from the British Museum down]

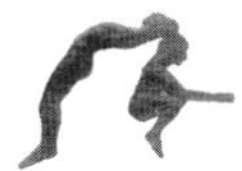

A figure from History class
I think we should retell it, to tell it again

[Tapping on the contact microphone on the glass table]

A story in which the cotton industry, rapping on doors, peddling door to door, is replaced by the printing of model clichés on fabric – or not.

[Contact microphone off]

A story's narrations are being told layer by layer. A certain time coincides with another, falls into another. In the statistics you are named, as one of many.

The existence of a person is defined by its silhouette. Her position in space. If she casts a shadow, what about empathy when she is having a chat with a silhouette? If out of that a figure emerges. A figure of speech or an image caption. One that circulates in our memory. Because you told it like that to me, and I imagine and compile myself out of that image.

[Pictures of silhouettes from the British Museum]

– a to c: A hole in my past; but you, you are from here?

I remember red benches, from the village improvers. Benches on which one can sit, enjoying the improved landscape, letting one's neutral gaze glide over the neutral landscape, to form, to educate a self. Redlining others, because of educational differences.

It's from there you can see the green border.
– a to b: I am falling
– b: You fall

One talks, the others listen.
Talking along, never about.

I finally find one of your sentences. I embed it between mine.
Signs mark, what is being joined and in which way.

[Placing quotation marks, commas, footnotes and brackets on the glass]

How do you like it, here with me, the way I typed you out and inserted
you, into this narration, this text.

An approach.
Approaching what?
Who talks?

The sentence returns, coming to my mind again. You said it here in this
room, the room was painted white. The sentence stayed with me, the
way you said it to me, in front of this wall, without having me in mind.
The sentence stayed with me. I memorised the sentence, without taking
notice. Now, because this room reminds me of you, it reappears here
beside me.

Who is here in this room now.

Speaking in a way that resists being cut into a statement, to be cut into
a statment, in a way it was not meant to be montaged, just because the
breath left a little break between the words. A way of perceiving speech that
goes along the breaks. A way of speaking that groups around the breaks.

Words that move along – from one body to another

Words that dress. Dress in your voice – that is already tomorrow,
a completely different one.

– Is it okay if I now pitch your voice a bit?

Saying this word in an everyday tone: indicating, implying, further
entanglement.
Sequences of words, immesurable, keywords or discourse.
A reminder from afar that it has been exactly like that – never trust
the witnesses; they usually invent what they have seen, without being
aware of it.

*– c: I do not find anything about you in the archives, the witnesses
   are all dead.*

Replacing the claim with an assumption.

What is happening between a recording for and the recording of.

Quietly pronouncing the words whilst typing them, checking if the
rhythm is unexpected. Whilst copy pasting – you can call it for quoting
if you wish – improvising the tone of other people's voices.

– On the basis of whom people build up in the footnotes.
*– Between that sentence and those, I embed mine, that is actually,
   a passed-on one.*

The original voice and the audio quote.

How a character can be distributed across several figures – where
quotation marks are set, which body, which sequence of steps, which
division of spaces.

*And even though, exactly that moment told in your words, could be
decisive.*

- *d: A narration that has slipped through between the keywords and their alphabetisation*

- *c is tired and would prefer to keep rehearsing tomorrow*

- *a and b are in urgent need of money and will go steal further figures at the colonial museum near by*

- *d would like to have a deeper voice in the next play, yet remain the same character*

[Fading out the contact microphone]

Text references

– Jürg Davatz, *Das Glarner Textilmuseum im Freulerpalast in Näfels* (Textile Museum of the Valley of Glarus in the Palace of Freuler in Näfels), 1989. '1740 a new industry in the Valley of Glarus began: textile printing. For the first time factories were founded. There existed important trade connections with Smyrna, Beirut, Constantinople, Varna among others. Design and colors had to correspond exactly to originals that were produced with simple means in their places of origin. Sales markets: Serbia, Bulgaria, Romania and Greece.' The designers of the cotton printing factories went to different regions in the Ottoman Empire, to find patterns and images that would help them to draw the printing templates according to the taste of their customers

– *Wirtschaftswachstum dank Sklavenhandel? Die Rolle Schweizer Akteure im transatlantischen Dreieckshandel im 17.- 19. Jahrhundert* (The role of Swiss actors in the 17th-19th century transatlantic trade triangle), cooperaxion, Bern 2013. 'Several printing factories sold their excellent batik products with great success to India and Indonesia, and later mainly to West Africa'

– Emil Zopfi, *Die Fabrikglocke* (The factory bell), Limmat Verlag, Zurich 2004. 'In 1837 the textile printing factory of Egidius Trümpy installed a bell to announce the start of the working days clearly. The workers responded to that with the first factory strike in Switzerland. Finally, in 1846 a decree for spinning mills was issued which limited the working day for children under 14 years to a maximum of 14 hours, and for everybody else to a maximum of 15 hours'

– Adolf Jenny-Trümpy, *Handel und Industrie des Kantons Glarus* (Trade and industry in the Canton of Glarus), Historischer Verein des Kantons Glarus, Glarus 1898. 'Wage labour by women and children was indispensable'

– Eva Maria Belser, *The White Man's Burden. Labour and Human Rights in a Globalised World*, Freiburg 2007. 'In the year of 1846 an initiative in Glarus was successful: Glarus was the first state in the world to introduce a factory decree, which determined a minimum age limit for children and also a limitation of working hours for adults'

– E-mail correspondences with Freulerpalast Näfels, 2013

Visual references

– 'Draft for a cloth in Turkey red with far eastern patterns' around 1835, in Jürg Davatz, cit.

A water canal above the Alps should have guaranteed access to sea trade routes. A train that is built instead and a solid statue that stays there unquestioned since, representing silent colonialisms in the name of progress and modernity. We hear three performers whose identities belong to facts as much as fantasy. Cross dressing, passing, questioning their rehabilitation in the name of ownership and naming.

The recorded voices can be heard from the museum's built-in speakers. The listeners are invited to move around. On the back of the script a silent sequence can be read, it is repoduced here on the margins of the page. A pyjama jacket and a free-hanging screen made of the same functional fabric. In the background one can see a terrace, the city, the lake of Lucerne and some mountains. Additional material: vinyls, audio advertisements, books, foldable tables and chairs, post boxes, marzipan fruits from the Caredda pastry shop.

[Playing *Flights of Fancy* by Maggie Payne]

How did you come to this place? By boat or by foot,
on water or land – and under which name? Were
you profiled by skin colour, asked about your sex,
your sexuality? Your income, your bank account?

First I have to say: it's not me, even if it's me, who
is announced with my name today, who wears my
name today, this functional pyjama, even if this is
my balcony furniture and my friends that comment
on the performance from afar.

[Moving the balcony table]

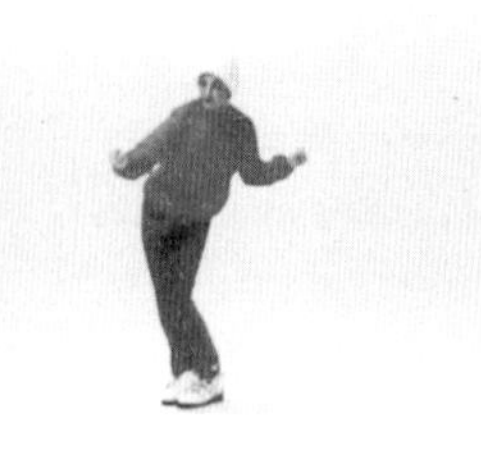

Jeanne Baret, what are you doing here? Are you mistaken in place and century ? Or are the biologists mistaken?

I forgot something.
I forgot a part of myself out there.
I don't know if I can go get it now.

Just now

Jeanne Baret is rediscovered as discoverer.

The logic of discovery has been reversed. It goes on and on – even if, there is nothing left to be named, measured, mapped, filed into lists and letter cases. In former times it was the continents, the plants. Nowadays it is the formerly unnamed.

[Playing *Furia* by The Fates]

Are You an
Underground?
A Ship's Deck,
or a Terrace.

'My first letters double-u have never been known. I am not in your history, your heart or your soul. Your paintings and pictures don't show my real face.'

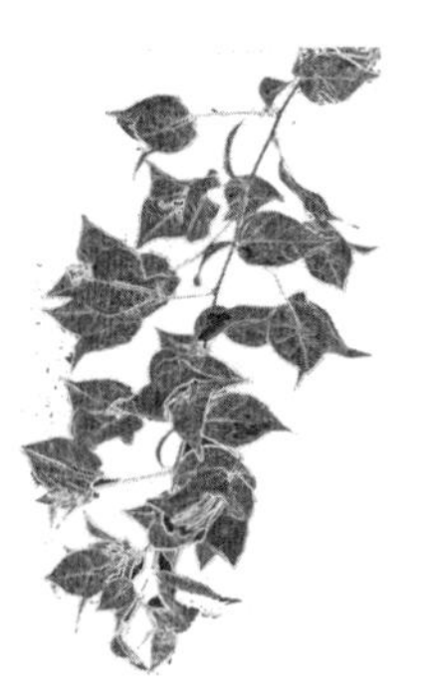

This is a bougainvillea, a plant that grows mostly in the southern hemisphere and also in Italy. Jeanne Baret, as Jean Baré, discovered it under the name of her partner Philibert Commerson during the expedition of Bougainvillea in South America. Her story is delivered to us in fragments by Denis Diderot alias Captain Jackson and is staged today as an interruptive meeting with the pirate and cross-dresser Mary Read.

[Lights on]

Just now, as privacy over sleeps, as I sublet my apartment, as I sell my name on the dark net –

Just now

Just now a canal is being drilled into the Alps with a gigantic drill bit. Another channel, through which those can operate and associate, that can move into any direction, if they so choose – completing a project from the 19th century.

For people: from north to south and back. For people camouflaged as goods: also in the opposite directions.

Just now, they are drilling away my window blinds, the railings. The balcony is rendered unusable, whereabouts to put the view, the balcony furniture? The drill is so loud that it seems as if they would drill the new Gotthard base tunnel across my room, even though I live on the third floor.

I have to shield you from the construction works with curtains. The first time it happens that the world of drilling and construction forces its way into my dreams, I am still laying in bed, and you with me.

Just now –
the discoverer Jeanne Baret is rediscovered.

[Playing *Running* by Delia Derbyshire]

'*The Dreeeaammss.*'

'Engineers that came back from the colonies, who had built big waterways and harbour projects there, wanted to connect and open Central Europe with the same means.'

Just now –

Just now, as the private slips into sleepiness, as I sublet my apartment, as I sell my name on the dark net – he (Escher) looks down his railway line from the station square towards the south.

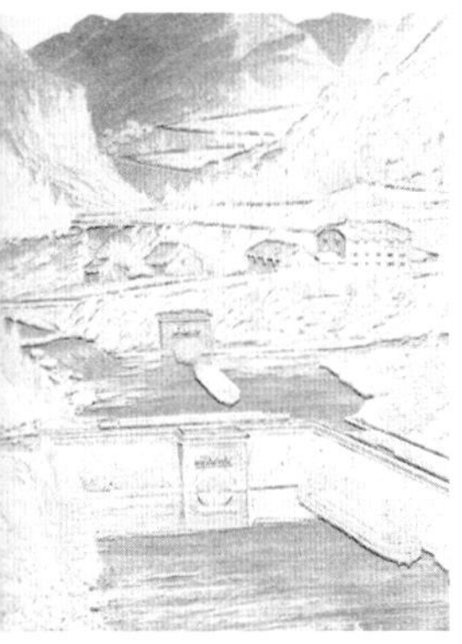

Free View of the Mediterranean

View of a lake that is supposed to be the sea.

In two hours and forty minutes one will be able to reach Milan from Zurich, through the new tunnel, with the new train, through the other even newer tunnel. Now we are all drilled awake, so we can connect, we from here.

'A journey from the grey North to the blue South has always been the dream of many people.' The Railway company advertises the new railway tunnel through the Alps.

The train is fast, but not for everyone.

Awake in a Dream   [Taking off the pyjama jacket]

I live here now. I brought along my balcony furniture, my curtain, my books, my multi-functional
pyjamas. I am ready for everything. At home we
are always ready for everything – ever since the
private became political.

This is the itinerary of Bougainvillea's ship, on
which Jeanne Baret was also on board. She circum-
navigated the world on this ship. Here to be seen as
a sustained line.

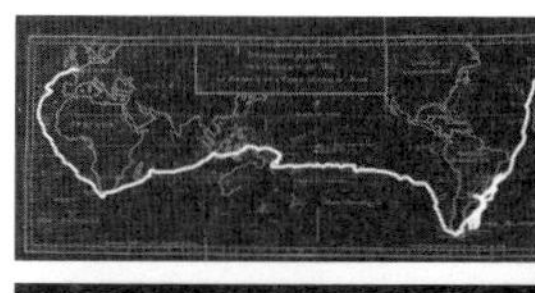
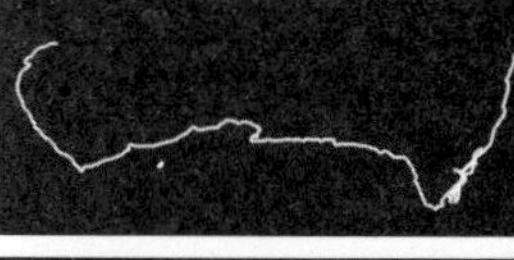
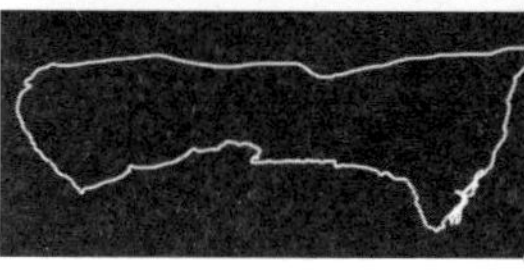

That's all we know about her, actually.

How is your view, your perspective? How is your life
being administered? How do you live your life? More
so in the form of a vanishing line? Or in a circle?

[Addressing the public]

You enter history here. Even though you have
already been my view for nearly 20 minutes.

With Fake Names

As whom or what do you pass? Did you drop out
as a woman and return as a man? Did you hijack a
name? For which underground, which tunnel, do
you work? Do you chose direct resistance or rather
the third way?

How did you come to this place? Did you come by
boat, across that sea, or on the land way, by foot?
And will you stay?

To move on water, on land, along hopes and promises.
It happens quite often that one loses orientation on
the open sea; the reflections of the water, the silhou-

ettes that dissolve in the night. The train on the contrary follows a direct line, one which only has two directions. The train is fast, but not for everyone. The train crosses the border in Chiasso. The Schengen agreement, the free movement of people? Train by train, the border guards draw the same invisible border – a racialized colour line.

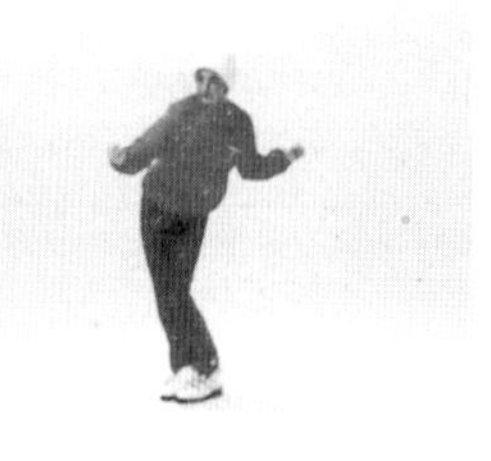

In the meantime Jeanne Baret is being made a woman again, for the discoveries that she made as Jean Baré. If he would agree with that?

'The only image we have of Jeanne Baret is an engraving by an unknown artist, published in Milan ten years after her death. She wears a loose jacket that has the same colour as her surroundings and her pants.'

This is all we know about him.

By Ship to Italy?

Crossing the Gotthard by train, reaching another scenery, one that resembles the Mediterranean.

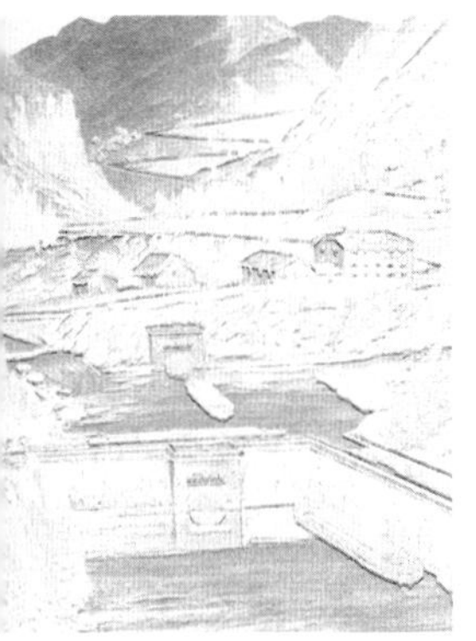

'Nobody expressed the objection, that it is completely absurd to cross the Alps with ships.'

On the way from Zurich to Naples, along the directed path surveyed by constructors of the railways, seeking connections to cotton production and the sea, we need a break.

A break that disturbs this narrative of progress and inclusion. Figures that intervene into the order of knowledge and how they are being told. Figures that join forces rather than fighting each other.

*I told them my body is a book and
they can ship me through as a
book, as a good.*

*I told them my body is a place for
social interruption and not for
reproduction
and they can ship
me through as a good.*

Around Lucerne the viscose industry is flourishing.   Figures that Intervene
Clothing for every weather, every life situation, is
produced in Emmenbrücken. Because the water
canal above the Alps will no longer be constructed,
they switch over to producing functional clothes for
ski tourism. Just in time for the first landing on the
moon and the rise of Science Fiction.

With piracy, hacking and the hijacking of names
and body shapes, Viscosuisse does not want to be
related to, and therefore withdraws retrospectively
from, the sponsoring of this scene, that took place
as the restaging of a sea battle during the festivities
of Lucerne Tourism last year.

Jeanne Baret, are you here?   Hacking

Symbolic Orders

Jeanne Baret: as Jean Baré, member of the explorative
expedition by Louis Antoine de Bougainville from
1766 to 1769, on board the ships La Boudeuse and
L'Étoile in the South Atlantic and the South Pacific.
His discoveries becoming known under the name
of his partner Philibert Commerson.

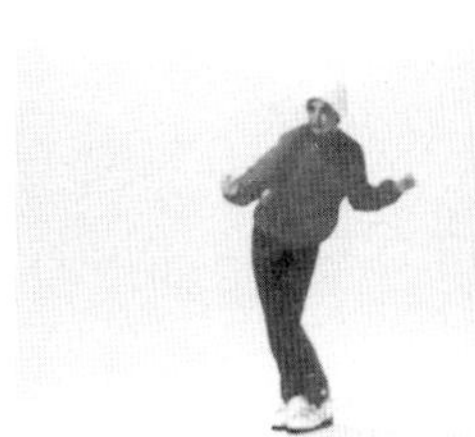

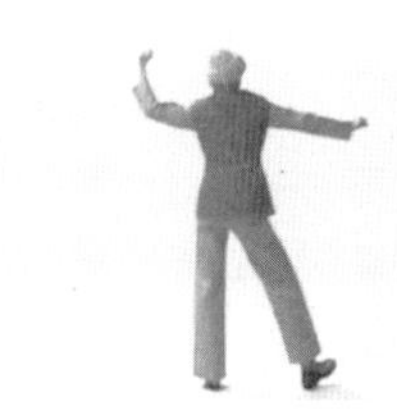

Mary Read: alias Mark Read, was an English pirate that operated in the Caribbean.

He and…

…Anne Bony were the most famous pirates during the golden age of analogue piracy.

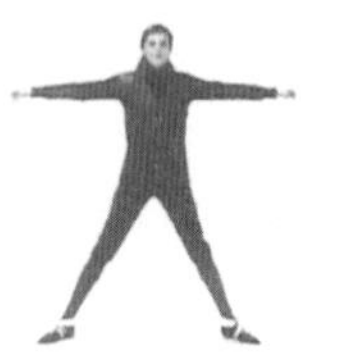

'What happens to marginalized memories, excluded from the valued usable past?'

Hacking the Social

Interrupting our view of the lake and this piece taking place, Mary Read, Anne Bony and Jeanne Baret discuss on the deck of their ghost ship, how to react to their rediscovery and rehabilitation by today's scientists. This time they are not covered, but rediscovered. They are needed now, urgently! Nightshades are named after them, romantic novels are written speculating about their lives; wild fantasies inhabit these biographies. As whom, by whom and for what purpose this time?

And we need
And we need
Mary Read

Passing

What do you mean by illegal! Just a few years ago they rehabilitated the escape agents from the Second World War and the witches from the Middle Ages. And now, closed down. And the history books too, now that we've realised how much is missing in there.

The borders: are being closed. Which means:
reopened, rebuilt. Along a white supremacist
perception of skin colour, the travellers are being
profiled. Which means controlled, in these direct,
always more direct trains. The ones that pass
keep quiet, looking out the windows as if there
was anything to be seen at the station of Chiasso,
despite a fortress-like underpass.

When anyone wants to leave the train, they do it on   **Passing that Eye**
their own, there is no need so be asked of your name.

The festivities of the rediscovery of Jean Baré as
Jeanne Baret are interrupted by the events of this
summer, whilst we try to see his biography as an
interruption of directed narratives.

Generally everything is in a muddle. Jeanne Baret
and Mary Read never met. Anna Bony on the contrary was in love with Mary Read. The three of them
have become female icons of gender mainstreaming.
They are listed on Wikipedia under false names.

[Playing *Estrogen* by Ravioli Me Away]

'*I wanna be a feminist but I don't know what it
means. Baby tell me what it means, baby tell me
what it means. Because many look just like me, I can
see them in my dreams, baby tell me what it means,
baby tell me what it means...*'

This is how I remember it:

There was music and three figures on a terrace, in a secret talk. Someone had just built a ferris wheel where the view of the lake was supposed to be. Because of this, listening was made difficult to. Outside, it was snowing already, even though you started your journey dressed as Jean Baré on a beautiful autumn day. In the backlight only silhouettes were recognisable. Silhouettes state the presence of a person, say Argentinian historians, who deal with finding evidence for the disappeared.

To occupy a name in the way one occupies a house.

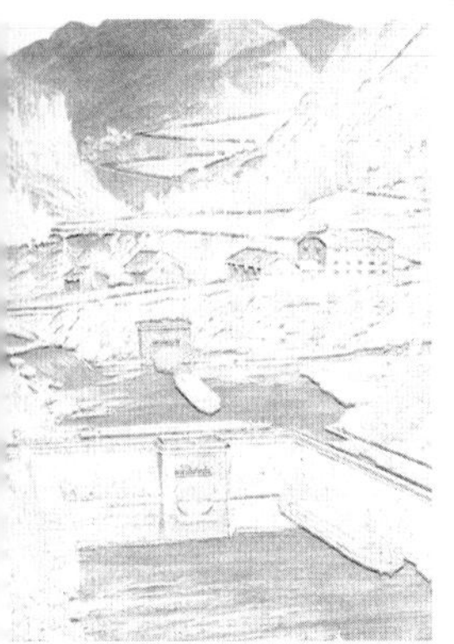

You can sleep here if you want, I can offer you this wonderful view. I am still in my pyjamas. If you want, we can talk about your journey and about mine too. We can exchange clothes, names, nationality. My siblings have been informed; we are experienced with death in this region – the death of technocrats at least. The death of those who built colonial projects in order to make views like this exist. 'Il colonialismo felpato', the silent colonialism, you know.

To move on water, on land, along hopes and promises. It happens quite often that one loses orientation on the open sea. The surface reflects, body shapes dissolve.

The train on the contrary follows a directed aim. To get closer to the sea calls for waterways, it is said until 1950 still.

In two hours and forty minutes one is supposed to
reach Milan from Zurich with the new train, the
always newer train, through the new tunnel, the
other even newer tunnel. We are all awake from the
drilling now, to be able to connect, 'we from here'.
The train is fast but not for everyone.

The train crosses the border in Chiasso. Along their
understanding of skin colours the border police
construct their border line.

What is this gaze that rambles?   **Multi-directional**
                                                     Time Machines

We have to find witnesses, to invent them or
be them ourselves. A search image, to the past,
something that is told, something that is described.

But you were there!

How can someone disappear if they have not yet   **A Vitesse**
appeared?   **Supersonique**

We find: letters, descriptions, an invoice, a note.
A recipe. Pressed and dried plants.

In the end, I cannot tell you everything; the pro-
ceedings are ongoing. Also for the protection of
witnesses.

Cross-Dressing &
Phytotherapy

The performance that I am talking about – I haven't seen it myself. A friend told me about it, asserting:

But you were there.

The way I remember it: there was music, three figures that intervened, in a secret talk on the terrace.

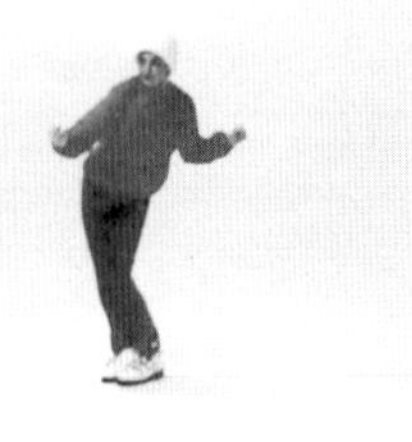

Cross-dressers, cross lovers
Cross readers, cross thinkers
You, your clothes, your dresses
The way you move your head
The way you say pity
In the moment I decide to go
What fiction do you wear today
Is it a scientific fiction
A feminist fiction, a grayscale fiction
A lost-eyed fiction
How is your cross-dressing going today

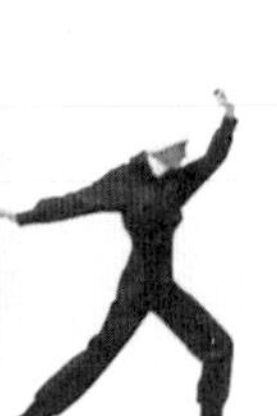

Passing

Just as I discover how Jeanne Baret discovers your favourite flower, the bougainvillea as Jean Baré in South America – I am searching for it in the botanical garden and in the library.

Was I awake or was I dreaming?

I have been drilled awake. A few days later, someone rings my doorbell. The post boxes will also be replaced, and they offer that I can choose a new tag, a new name.

If I would have sold my name a while ago, this apartment would have been sublet by now, I would already feel I do not exist anymore. Now how might I find myself: from here, allowed to vote, legal, working, paid.

Sleeping in a name, eating in another, loving with a third, working without.

To make an event exist, it must first circulate. We have to find witnesses or invent them or be them ourselves. A search image to the past, something that is told, something that is described.

[Playing *Flights of Fancy* by Maggie Payne]

I told them my body is a book and they can ship me through as a book, as a good.

I told them my body is a place for social interruption and not for reproduction.

Free Passage
through the
Mediterranean

Note

The definition of 'silent colonialism' (colonialismo felpato) refers to entrepreneurs from St. Gallen and Zurich that introduced industrial cotton spinning mills in the two Sicilies around 1800. Also because of the possibility to grow cotton plants in the South of Italy – and therefore bypassing Napoleon's continental blockage and trade embargo for cotton from the Americas. The industrialists profited from the political system of the region and exploited the local workforce without initiating or en-abling a transfer of knowledge and technologies. The machines were brought and installed by Zurich based engineering company Escher Wyss.

Text references

- Daniele Mariani, *Imprenditori svizzeri alla conquista del sud* (Swiss enterpreneurs conquesting the South), 2011. swissinfo.ch
- Lorenzo Zichichi, *Il colonialismo felpato*, Sellerio Editore, Palermo 1988
- Andreas Teuscher, *Schweiz am Meer*, Limmat Verlag, Zurich 2014. 'Nobody said that it was completely absurd to cross the Alps by ship.' Repatriates from the colonies wanted to apply the idea of total control over landscape in Central Europe. That's how the idea to build a canal that would cross the Alps became a fantasy of how to guarantee a connection to the sea
- Mickael Augeron et Robert Duplessis, *Fleuves, rivières et colonies*, les indes savantes, Paris 2010. 'Waterways – particularly but not exclusively rivers – became organizing metaphors for colonization, images of novelty, of promise, and also of threat. They were emblematic of strategic possibilities that metropolitan authorities sought to exploit, of the mastery of space that colonizers sought to achieve, of the markets that manufacturers and merchants sought to develop, of the riches that colonists sought to attain. They represented, too, a rich array of imaginative resources for artists, intellectuals, and academics – and have remained so, for good and for ill, for exploring new understandings and for reiterating hoary stereotypes, until today'
- Glynis Ridley, *The Discovery of Jeanne Baret. A Story of Science, the High Seas, and the First Woman to Circumnavigate the Globe*, Broadway Books, New York 2011. 'The systematic exclusion of woman from the field of taxonomy is so much a part of Baret's story that the historical silence surrounding her cannot fully be explained without understanding something of taxonomy's history. […] The only image we have of Jean Baret is an engraving by an unknown artist, published in Milan ten years after her death. She wears a loose jacket that has the same colour as her surroundings and her pants.' 'She told Bougainville that she was 26, orphaned, born in Burgundy.' 'The knowledge about plants was passed on by mothers to their daughters: it was normal, that rural women had this expertise.' 'After 250 years the exploits of French plant hunter Jeanne Baret are being recognised by naming a nightshade in her honour.' 'The principle of priority has not always been the modus operandi for naming' 'Nieder mit den Alpen. Freie Sicht auf's Mittelmeer' (Away with the Alps. Open up the view to the Mediterranean) was the slogan of the Zurich Youth Movement in 1980. The uprisings went against the establishment, and claimed cultural freedom and cultural centres (kultureller Freiraum), and a redistribution of cultural funding

– 'Nieder mit den Alpen. Freie Fahrt durch's Mittelmeer' (Away with the Alps. Free passage through the Mediterranean) is the adaptation of the slogan by activists, pointing towards the 'Fortress Europe policy' as acted out by Frontex in 2015
– Alliance against Racial Profiling, *Alternative Report on Racial Profiling. Practice of the Swiss Police and Border Guard Authorities*, Switzerland May 2017. 'Recent research shows that Black people, People of Colour, Yenish people and Roma people in Switzerland are exposed to widespread, recurrent, and often humiliating police checks. […] There is also increasing criticism from attorneys and legal scholars of systematic and deliberate racial profiling practices against Roma, Sinti and Yenish on Swiss territory as well as against Black people and people with a North African or Slavic appearance at the Swiss border in Como/Chiasso'

Sound references

– *Who am I?* by The Fates, in 'Furia', LP 1985
– *Flights of Fancy* by Maggie Payne, in 'Ahh-Ahh (Music For Ed Tannenbaum's Technological Feets 1984-1987) ', LP 2012
– *Estrogen* by Ravioli Me Away, in 'The Inevitable Album', LP 2014
– *Running* by Delia Derbyshire & Barry Bermange, in 'Inventions For Radio. The Dreams', LP 2014. Originally broadcasted on BBC radio in 1964

Visual references

– Figures in red, yellow and blue functional wear by Viscosuisse, Emmenbrücken 1974
– Placeholder figures for Jean Baré, Mary Read, Anne Bony are stills from a TV commercial by Viscosuisse, Emmenbrücken near Lucerne, ca. 1950 (Archive of Viscosuisse at State Archives Lucerne)
– The Statue of Alfred Escher at Zurich's main station square. Escher was an entrepreneur and a politician. He inherited a fortune. His father owned a.o. a slave plantation in Cuba. Escher founded all the institutions needed to build the Gotthard tunnel: a credit bank, a re-insurance company, a technical university and a railway company

Two suffragette women cross-dressing on a journey in their photostudio in Horten, Norway. Their images have been rediscovered recently and re-circulated by researchers and artists. More and more voices join them: records, entire playlists, friends, groups and their personal memories, also birds, an entire record store. Their boat goes along with musical vocabularies, through the store's categories, searching for Amazons in Amazonia. They float along the description of a paradise in the 'new world', losing each other in a very long Loa, a jocular introduction used in theatres during the Siglo de Oro (or Spanish Golden Age). A performance on love, friendship and former selves. There are two ways to follow the performance: From inside the venue as a listener or through its window as a spectator. Silent sequences were printed on the backside of the script. A fictive tracklist was announced per invitation mail.

[The projection shows a few introductory notes]

According to the movement of her eyes

The murderer: writing like loving needs a motive

Imagining past sounds while casually listening to ongoing ones

Language is a skin. I rub my language against the other

The idea of a sound recording the exact moment of its taking

I don't like your tone, I like your tone, I like the tone of this place

Directed by Direct Democracy.
Directly excluding democratically.
I will never stop lifting up all these Masks.
Claude Cahun said

**From Monte Carlo
to Kirkuk**

A and Âif, Anifen and Bali, Bali and Brassens

Reportages about the women of the Kurdish
Peschmerga fighters have filled the summer lull.
Suddenly no longer seen as members of a terrorist
organisation, but featured as heroines of gender-
mainstreaming. As heroines of the West too.

This is an issue I would like to discuss with Marie
Høeg and Bolette Berg. But it seems they are not
reachable at the moment, probably in a spot in the
Amazon with no reception, escaping recent rumours
about their afterlife career.

Workers and Lovers

The mockery of integration

To fill the autumn lull the newspapers are back to
local politics: The Federal Council's sudden com-
mitment to the integration of women into the work
process.

Since last week, this integration is of high importance for the politicians.

Now, that it will no longer be possible to call for the
missing manpower, which means people, according
to desire and mood, according to demands, which
means: as required. The referendum of last spring.
The ecopop-initiative of this autumn.

Now the politicians really sat down and deliberated and discovered a missing resource: women. Which means: still to exploit, still under control. The woman as the new economic power, which means: gap-fillers. Now this woman – she who just dropped out – enters, steps in, runs. Runs – according to the newspapers – after the five new places in daycare to later run for that running economy. She who dropped out. She who protests against such and other colonial thoughts and misogyny, denying all categories.

It looks like war. Are we in a war? A war industry with outsourced death. The work does not seem to run dry, only the workers.

In semi-darkness we hear some voices: we are standing at the Orinoco river [volume of birds twittering increases] *the thing with the Orinoco river is this…* [volume of birds twittering increases] *Field Recordings… Women in Music… WIM… Max Havelaar…*

Headbang against Ecopop

Did she say someting about Max Havelaar? Fair Trade? Trade? Is that fair? Is it fair that goods but not the people producing them can cross these borders, is this fair? Is it fair compared to Fair Trade?

[Records are placed in shop windows by artists intervening into the tightening asylum politics of recent years]

    Discoveries and ownership

[Playing *Beings That Accept and Embrace the Growth of Other Beings*]

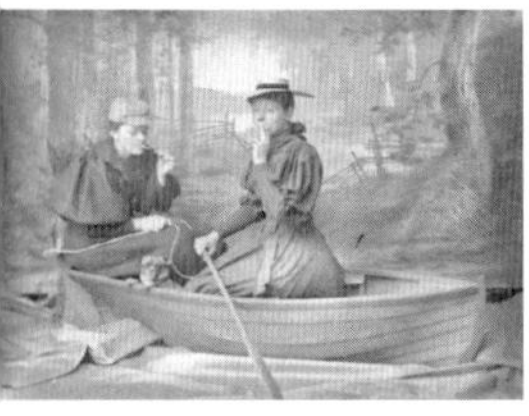

Yesterday we redirected the Orinoco river into the Amazon to reach a fluent narration. We boated along the Amazon searching for the Amazons. Marie Høeg, Bolette Berg and I.

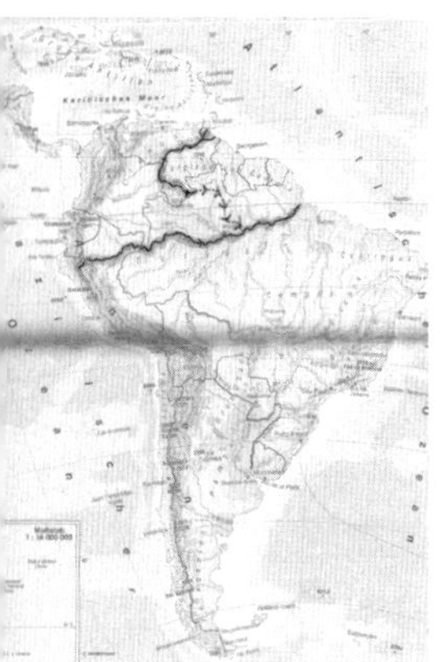

Along the course of the Amazone – the shape it had during the Golden Age – we introduced the Loa as form. A form that emerged during the continuous age of golden exploitation. Golden for the exploiters, that is clear.

Due to lacking knowledge of the Spanish language and bad sources, Marie Høeg and Bolette Berg, amongst many explorers of that time, confuse the occidental with the oriental India.
It's not such a problem for them, since they are only staging this journey for the camera – in their photo studio in Horten.

Berg falls in love with an Amazon and leaves Høeg. A few month later Marie Høeg writes her famous speech for women's suffrage.

[Reading Marie Høeg, *Women and the Right to Vote*]

Today hopefully, she would say the same, as a women who is not allowed to vote, due to her residence status or missing papers.

Women and the Right to Vote.
Lecture by Marie Høeg on the occasion of the women's meeting in Horten Norway, November 1901

'The right to vote is a means, the only means, that gives the simple individuum the possibility to influence the society, its promises and visions of the future. All the ones, who stay silent in their discrimination, all the ones who suffer in some way under the common social order, can find a means in the right to vote to work against these disadvantages that are opressing them. We have to understand the power that lais in the right to vote and how precious this right actually is.

We understand now how crazy it is, that this right has been refused to half of the population, that it lied in the hands of men alone, whilst women have been excluded from political rights and participation. These women are not only interested in care taking – an interest that coincides with the interest of men – they have a special interest in care taking.

This is why women's suffrage is not an intervention into the rights of men. But the privilege of men to vote, was an intervention and an injustice towards the human rights of women.'

Signifier and signfied

Speaking as, speaking about

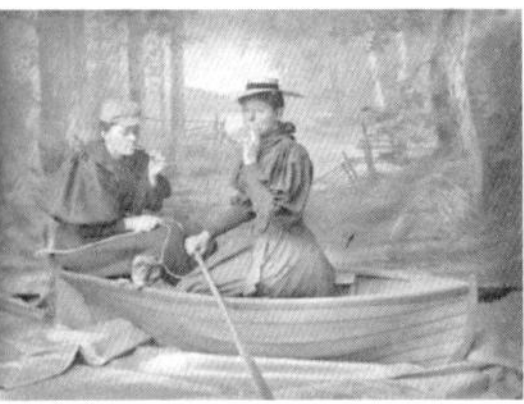

In the first scene during their search for the Amazon in Amazonia Marie Høeg and Bolette Berg follow inconsistent sources. One of them is a book by Antonio de León Pinelo, who tries to locate the paradise along the rivers in South America.

[Reading Antonio de León de Pinelo, *El Paraíso en el Nuevo Mundo*]

'Concerning the discussed six arguments, the paradise might be found in oriental India. But I will describe why the paradise might be located in occidental India.'

'Some women in occidental India live in self-governed communities: without communicating with or being supported by men. This is why they can be called Amazons.'

'When they give birth to a boy, they send him to his father. If it is a girl, they keep it in their community.'

'Some Amazons live along the Orinoco river.'

'These grounds were taken by women, the way ancient Amazons used to live. And they are very very rich, they own a lot of gold and money, and they have houses that are completely covered with gold.'

Every connection is constructed. Sometimes even landscapes are redesigned by description. In our case we redirected the Orinoco river into the Amazon to reach a fluent narration.

[Fading out the record playing in the back ground]

As Bolette Berg is saying this, Marie Høeg is already changing clothes for the day's next staging. She wears a fur that covers her body entirely and the stiff gaze of discoverers and inventors.

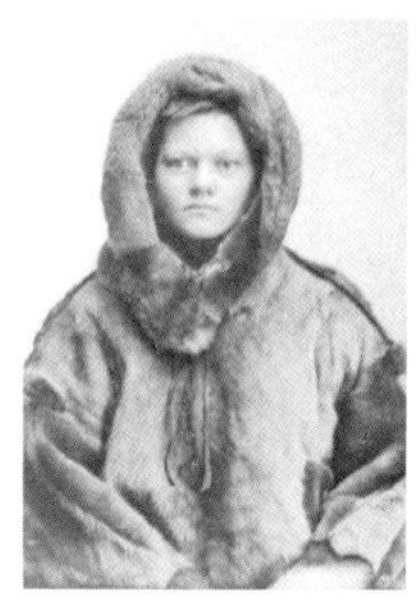

Mi amor se fue y yo me quedé
In Spanish it sounds better

Going away whilst others stay

The Loa is a variation of the prologue, that came up during the 'Siglo de oro', the Golden Age. Golden because Europe was enrichening and establishing itself thanks to the exploitation of the recently discovered colonies. This also led to flourishing in the arts. The Loa is one of them.

The Loa deals with everyday stuff, Asuntos Profanos. The actors introduce themselves. The patron is shamelessly praised. Financial dependencies are commented upon. This form of the prologue was called for Loa and was seen as a necessary part of a performance to make the plot understandable. The Loa was not part of this plot, but a short summary of the plot. One of the first Loas is called 'Amor aumenta el valor' (Love makes things more valuable). The piece begins with voices getting closer in the dark.

[Playing *Beings That Accept and Embrace the Growth of Other Beings*]

The Queen of Your Heart

This scene takes place during Marie Høeg and Bolette Berg's journey across the Amazon: Marie Høeg looses Bolette Berg because she falls in love with an Amazon whilst intervening in a rape scene described by Elizabeth Bishop, taking place in 1502.

It is also possible that Berg fell out of the boat and Marie Høeg tells the story the way she does, so that she doesn't have to explain why and how Berg actually fell out of the boat.

Bolette Berg has drowned. That now seems clear. What we have are pictures of the two women in which they are staging themselves as discoverers and other typically male-gendered characters. The discovery of such pictures is nothing new. But because they are rediscovered, once again this discovery is valuable.

A continued Age
of self-gilding
Exploitation

Tired and bad mooded in the record store

The Loa was spoken in simple verses that everybody could understand. Verses familiar to other short forms of theater such as the Entremes. New forms were developed out of them, such as the Dialogical Loa or the Loa Entremesada, the Loa of Bits. 'The Loa Entremesada was embodied by different characters as minimal actions. The Loa Cortesana would shamelessely praise the rich, who had financed the performance, to comment on interdependencies. Because the travelling theater groups had no printed programs, they also used the Loa to introduce the actors. The Loa had a meta-function as part of the theater piece. Later the Loa also included a short

summary of the comedy that served as an introduction.'

We are not Rydiard Kippling An Enclave of Utopia

*'The landscape was fantastic. This all has a western-
undertone, and I am sure that this counts.'*

To describe the work, the working conditions, love
under these working conditions.

Black outs and jeopardy Danger of Collusions

Uncover and Covering up.

- *I am looking for 'We Agree About Democracy. But
  What Do We Actually Agree About?'*
- *We don't have it*
- *But I could recommend 'We Don't Agree About
  Anything' by N.O. or 'The Universal Universality of
  the University of Human Rights'*

It is not very pleasant to be found out by a vinyl in Love after Midnight
one's private life, whilst groping in the dark with it. under a Sunset
by S. and M.

- *We have someone with very special interests here*
- There is not even a category that could define it

Does this mean it is not possible to find it?

Finding whilst inventing: for this we don't need a
category at all – finally!

Too high-tone for Gossip

Gossip in the city, chitchat in the countryside

Everything that happens behind one's back. Gossip is an underestimated currency. The Loa included it as a common repertoire.

'I love to write audio plays, because I love to write dialogues.'

Fag Hags in the Hinterland

Fag hags in the countryside
It does not have to be the Amazon necessarily

[Reading a snippet from 'Jungle World', 27 February 2014]

There is no commenting on the ongoing age of gilded exploitation in this article. Nor about the question of who can write whose history and be heard through whose words.

Love in the 1990s in the Villages

What we see:

Marie Høeg and Bolette Berg in a Boat in their studio in Horten

Marie Høeg as Fridtjof Nansen

The redirection of the Orinoco river into the Amazon

Hands, browsing the record store for answers,

rhythmically searching the script

A book by Antonio de León Pinelo

An article out of 'Jungle World'

A speech about women's suffrage by Marie Høeg

A CD 'Rock Down Aslygesetz'

'It does not have to be the Amazon necessarily. Literature should describe the world as it is. For this, some imagination might be necessary. Another comment on the debate about contemporary German literature.'

A Flexidisc by Joana Escoval

A laptop, a beamer, a vinyl player, a zoom

A new record store

Flyers and posters by Anna Frei

Franziska Koch recording, Michaela di Savino documenting

Neon lights by Lena Reiser, books by edition fink

The staging of Karen Geyer later performance

Someone stands by the window – that is me

In front of the window, people are watching

Someone is painting the sign for Straight Edge on her hands with a thick black marker. Luckily she didn't do it for real back then – if she had done so, she would say now it was because of Malcolm X

[Drawing Straight Edge signs (crosses) on hands]

Straight Edge and Vegan

All dressed in black with long black hair on the green countryside. All straight edge and vegan. Eating algas and sushi rolls.

Heavy Metal and all forms of love that do not exist in sexual education at school.

Quilts in the entrance hall, in memory of those who have died from AIDS. The first generation in the gymnasium, the first generation with sexual education – informing and norming them.
What does Maryanne Amacher know about love in the 1990s in the villages? Nothing. But she says that she likes the tone of that place. I say she said this and so I say it here. To make her be in this room.

'Spontaneous Colonisation' is written there. I don't know how to imagine a spontaneous colonisation and whether it is similar to a spontaneous robbery, a spontaneous visit, a spontaneous murder, a spontaneous assault.

Who cares
about Love in the
1990s in the
Villages anymore?

1. Go to the theater if you want to see a theater performance.

A Colony of
the Bourgeoisie

2. Who ever said a feminist performance has anything to do with the refusal of speech, expressive gesturing and nakedness. THIS IS WRONG!

3. To whoever is eager to see some naked skin: I can recommend the sauna at the lake.

4. Beneath all nakedness there are several organs that produce our speech.
It is there where words will find their way from one body to another. A happy epitome.

[Fading in William Onyeabor]

Smooth and good

'*When the going is smooth and good, many many people will be your friend*'

Notes

Loa: introduction, prolog, anouncement, short form, anecdote, comment, meta-text, summary of the plot, indication, gratitude.

Text references

– Marie Høeg, *Kvinderne og valget, Foredrag på Kvindemøtet* (Women and elections, Lecture in the women's meeting), in 'Gjengangeren', November 1901

– Antonio de León de Pinelo, *El Paraíso en el Nuevo Mundo. Comentario apologético. Historia natural, y peregrina de las Indias Occidentales, islas, de Tierra-Firme del Mar Occeano*, Madrid 1656

– Marguerite Duras, interview in *Worn Out With Desire To Write*, Argos Films, 1985. 'C'est une note occidentale. Et je sais que ça conte.'

Visual references

– Photograph of Marie Høeg and Bolette Berg in a boat on a journey in their photostudio, Horten 1900, as circulated on e-flux, 30 May 2014

– Photograph of Marie Høeg as the discoverer Fridtjof Nansen, Horten 1900

Sound references

– *Beings That Accept and Embrace the Growth of Other Beings* by Joana Escoval, Flexi-Disc 2009

– Conversation with Marie-Luise Kaschnitz, Hörspielarchiv SRF, Zurich 1969

It is getting late. Trying to reach feminist authors in Italy, who have been writing about the sexual difference in the 1970s. Following similarities in wording, the search leads from sexual difference to how differences appear as interlockers of matrixes of oppression (sexism, classism, racism) in intersectional feminism, and how difference is present in discourses around gender now. A play with words and trains of thoughts in reference to the self portraits, the images with fists and texts, the notes and the 'I' and 'You' of artist Ketty La Rocca.

In the background, projection subtitles start to move silently across the screen, along ghost hands and flickering fields, commenting on and affirming what is said. The performance calls and channels voices, repeating them according to recordings and printed scripts, assembling and distorting them.

[Fading in *Flights of Fancy* by Maggie Payne]
[On the projection in the back subtitles begin to move]

I		You.
I	see	You.
I	read	You.
I		You.

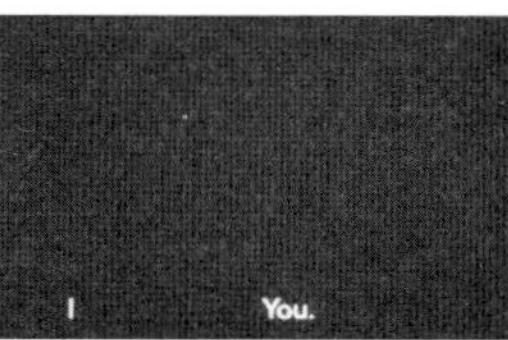

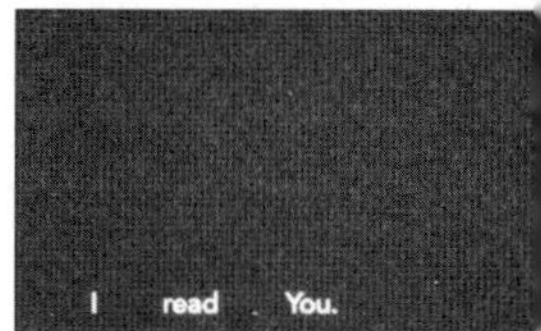

[Listening] What is underlined generates a line that connects places and names, emphasizes, picks out and highlights. It's the thread of one of many possible memories. How many coded languages do you speak and how many do you write? This is a history of ghost writers and aliases, publishing under false names, readings between the lines, social codes and visual ones. The line which I am speaking along, is the silhouette of a shared body of thoughts. It's the line of people like you and me. Without place, without belonging. It's the memory of the material that words are made of and that makes them flow and change. Change meanings and associations. Outside of representational politics. Performative constellations don't stay. The words that this memory underlines, the underlinings that make me memorize, are passed from one hand to the other; it's an oral history, a physical history, a history of affects and of intimacy, outside the realm of kinship and collective memory. It's the underground. It's distributors are: everything a *white* publisher won't publish today. To believe and follow the essential and the authentic in the hegemonic patriarchal order, the attempt to complete a *white* avant-garde is also in the digital a way of deleting, ignoring, fading out, making invisible.

[On the projection in the back subtitles begin to move]

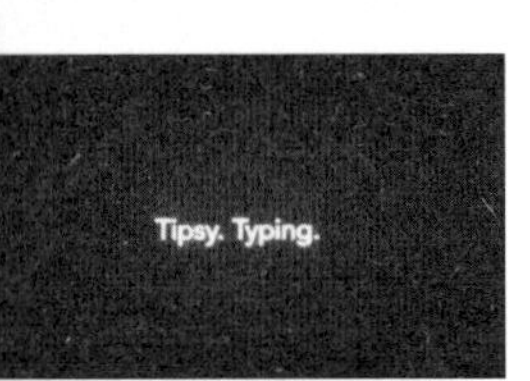

A hot summer night
The windows wide open

   Tipsy. Typing.

       Typing: The windows open.

I am thinking of   You.

The main, the centre, protagonists, figures, fists

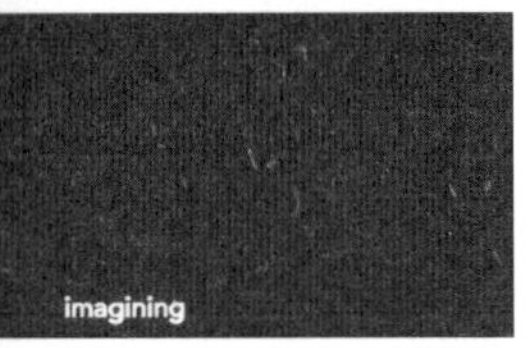

I   You.
    imagining
I   You.

A field without centre, antagonists, side figures, fists

So why not go into what we most fear:

difference

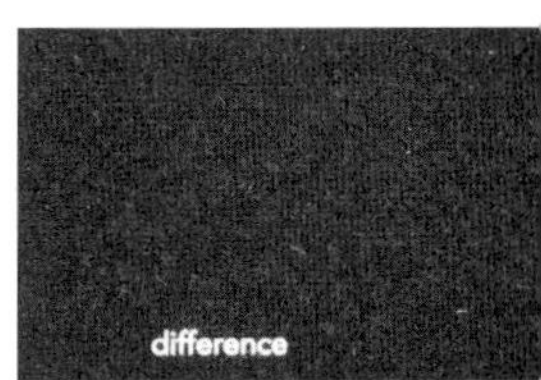

Personal Pronouns.
The personal and the political.
Possessive Pronouns.
Possessing. The own and the other.
The indexicality of the concrete poem.
Me and you. Cross dressing.
Cross dressing the symbolic order.

[Listenig] What can be read between the lines between the signs. It's a code outside the binary, it's a social code. Wording. *White.* Wording. Have you ever tried to google a text written by a no name only mentioning no names? Untagged, no keyword fitting? You won't find it. Estrogen. Long hair? Privilege. Testosterone. Soft hands. I am a ghost writer. I am a ghost. I do what most people don't like to do: I write. I can have any gender. What I do: writing for others, in the name of others.

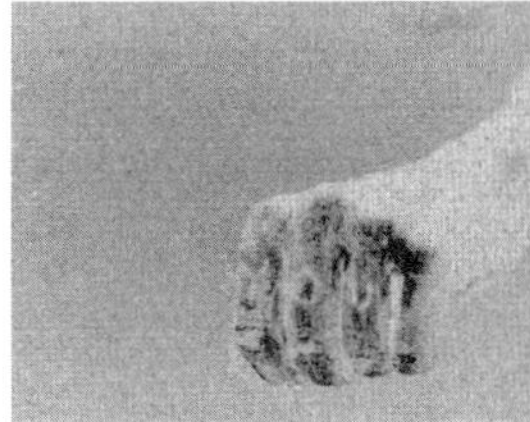

My words address a social code, I hack the social. Shifting the social order.

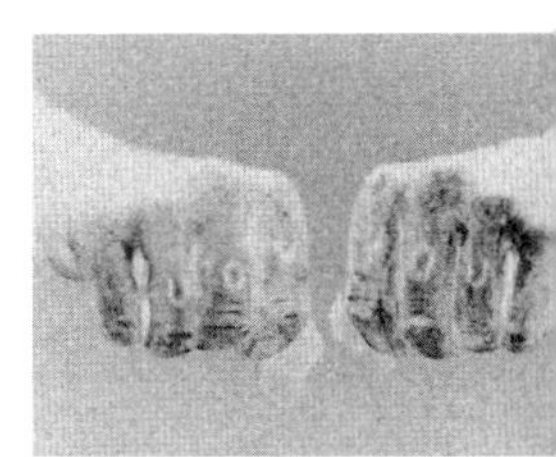

[Playing *Estrogen* by Ravioli Me Away]

'I wanna be a feminist

I don't know what it means

Estrogen, estrogen!'

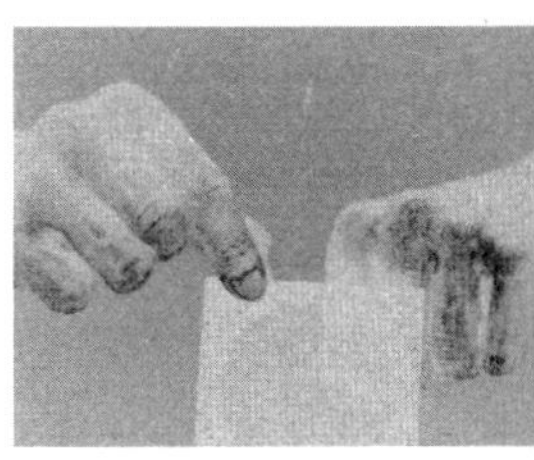

*For Rivolta Femminile the woman is not the object
of the image or the sentence, but the author and the
spectator of the artwork.*

[Reading] The I in question is an artist I
This I is somewhere between
The lived and the staged
Between the social and the symbolic order

I   You.

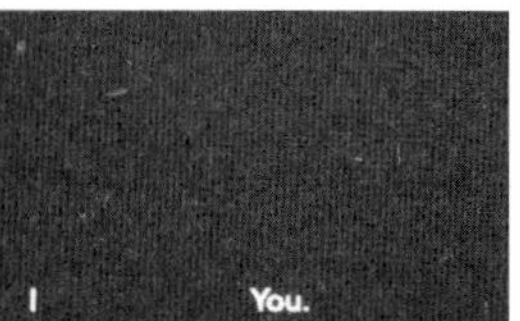

An order can be changed or abandoned

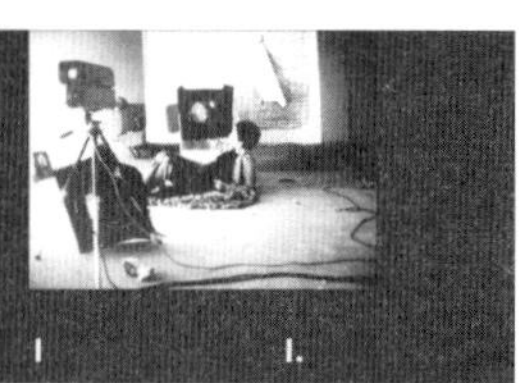

This I is an artist I
An I that asks for the possible I
A staged I, that counters the viewer's eye

This I becomes a performing I
and lies in bed with another I
That is: made out of plastic

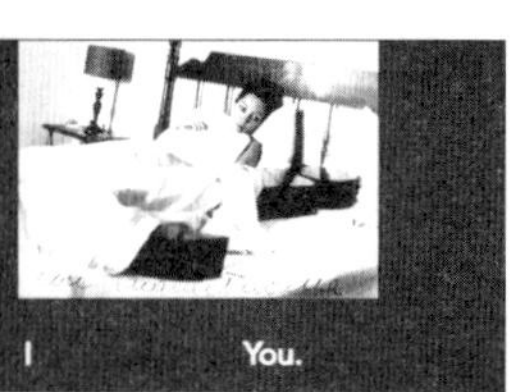

This artist performer I
lies in bed with an other I
That is: a sculpture
Staging a half-gendered couple
in a bourgeois bed
Taking the I literally,
concrete, visual, conceptual:
Taking the I as a signifier

The I of the alphabet

The I of the symbolic order

Taking the I as a signified

The I as a shape

The I of the artist

The I of a self-declared woman in Florence

in the 1970s

[Listening] Has the I of this artist in the bourgeois
bed, operating in the symbolic order, in Florence,
Italy, in the 1970s, got anything to do with the I of
the paisans and workers, operating in the social
order, leaving Italy to find temporary work in
Switzerland, in the same 1970s? They wrote, in a
manifesto of foreign women:

'(Also in Switzerland) we experience multiple disadvantages: as foreigners, as women, as mothers, as
workers.'

Has this I of an artist wanting to be perceived as an
artist in her time got anything to do with the I of
Carla Lonzi's 1970s in Italy in which she, the art
critic, would blame art as contaminated, as a tool
of the patriarchal system that had to be questioned
fundamentally and abandoned, when she would say:
'Io dico io.' I say I. Who said that ideology is also
my adventure? 'La mia avventura sono io.' My
adventure, that's me.

The I that wants to be perceived as an artist in the
1970s had first to agree with a system in which until
then women had mainly to be: woman.

And the role of this woman had to be turned around: from object to subject, from motive to an actor with agency.

The I in these 1970s feminisms is a fixed and essential entity, always opposed to a you: the you is now the I and the former subject the other. That can be: the male artist, the male lover, the male gaze, the main contradiction in marxism, the I of the liberal market.

[Listening] I run into Ketty La Rocca a hot summer night. The windows wide open. Typing: #Rivoluzione Femminile #il mio lavoro

I run into Ketty La Rocca, a bit tipsy, one hot summer night. Typing: visual poetry, the feminist revolution

I run into her, one hot summer night, it must have been late. Typing: conceptual art, privileges, literacy

I run into her, the temperature had dropped below 30 degrees, it must have been late. Typing: male gaze, photography, second wave feminism

I run into her, I was searching for role models for a performance, it must have been late. Typing: representation politics, subject object camera, feminist performance

I run into her, after my guests had left. Searching for: sisterhood, jealousy, say her name

I run into her, tired from the heat. Typing:
misogyny, hormonal therapy, bio power

I run into her, waiting for a phone call late at night.
The skype open, the sounds of people logging in
and out. Typing: read women, feminist fictions,
translation politics

I run into her, following a few tweets before falling
asleep, typing: longing for the longing, fuck the
privileged, desire for a past

[Reading] I met her late one hot summer night. Tipsy.
Typing: Italy, difference, feminism, art

I run into her one hot summer night. Typing:
Rivoluzione Femminile, work, social reproduction,
drop outs

[Sound effects on microphone, digital delay (on and off)]

I wanted to be intimate with her. She seemed so
lonely between all these men. Typing: feminism, the
sexual difference, differences, making differences,
doing differences

I wanted to be close to Ketty: I went looking for her
in the Libreria delle Donne, the women's library in
Milan, but there she wasn't around.

Instead I found her later in an exhibition called
'La Grande Madre', the great mother. Somehow it
didn't make any sense.

Somewhere in the heat of last summer, the heat in my apartment and the heat in my studio, I met her. Probably it's late and the temperature has dropped below 30.

I meet her through her work.
I meet her through my work. 'Il mio lavoro.'

I ask her if and how she is involved in the 'Rivoluzione Femminile' the Women's Revolution, a radical feminist movement in Italy connected to the art world of her time.

I invite her to our working group on feminist fictions to hear what she would say.
I ask her what she knows about Italian workers going from the South to work in the North, whilst she is teaching school kids for 'equality' as she writes, reading about the war in Vietnam, producing her work in Florence.

I ask her what she thinks about losing the mother and killing the father.

I ask her what she thinks about gender mainstreaming and the export of a western ideals of the liberated woman.

I meet her later that year again, in a book with her writings, published in Berlin.
She doesn't like to write she tells me.
But she writes: 'Ancora in Italia al meno, essere una donna e fare il mio lavoro è di una difficoltà

incredibile.' Still – at least in Italy – to be a woman
and to do my work is incredibly difficult.

The more time I spend with Ketty, the more I
realize that my wish for a past will stay unfulfilled.

[Sound effects on microphone, digital delay (up fast), on the
projection in the back subtitles begin to move]

I   hear   You.

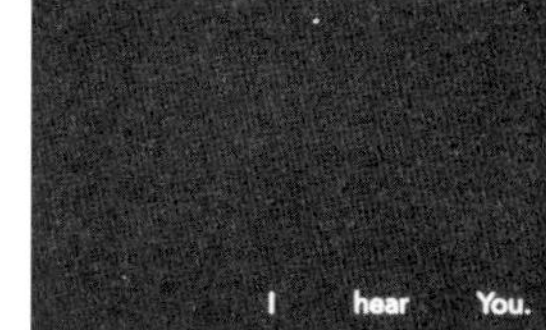

It's become late. Years off. Fighting. The patriarchal
system. The patriarchal understanding of culture,
of art. Art as. Art as avant garde. *White* middle
class male. Avant garde. This is a talk about white-
ness between *white* people. It's the white skin under
that light in the night.

It's become late. We speak about sexual difference
and heterosexual sexuality. We speak about an understanding of culture, that leaves most of culture
and its actors out. Out of sight.

It's become late that summer night. In the
darkroom. Out of sight. Red light. In the darkroom.
Developing. Dark and analogue – photography.

I had the feeling that we kept talking. I began to
understand her work, and I had the feeling she
didn't understand mine. I don't read German, she
would say.

The desire for having a past
Many of them

You the protagonist
I the externalized voice
You the I of that protagonist
I the cross dresser

You the antagonist
I the digitized
You the past of my desire
I the I in the you

You the fist in the eye
Assembled out of all these voices
The techno changes
Nothing changes

Slightly change
Change your name every day
Change address
Change pronoun
Change partners

Change Responsibilities
Dissolve
Digitized
Quantized
You

[Sound effects on microphone, digital delay]

[Reading] I am invited to meet someone. A feminist artist from the 1970s, they say. A feminist artist from the 1970s is as if you would say: a feminist artist from the 1970s.

We seemingly know what this artist would say:

[Sound effects on microphone digital delay]

'Ancora, in Italia almeno, essere una donna e fare il mio lavoro è di una difficoltà incredibile.' Still – at least in Italy – to be a woman and to do my work is incredibly difficult.

[Digital delay (up and off)]

I keep my body out. Out of light, out of sight, out of discussion. I say I.

Fists, two of them.

Fists, in the brain.

Fists up in the air.

Fists, in the 1970s is a sign.

[On the projection in the back subtitles begin to move]

differences

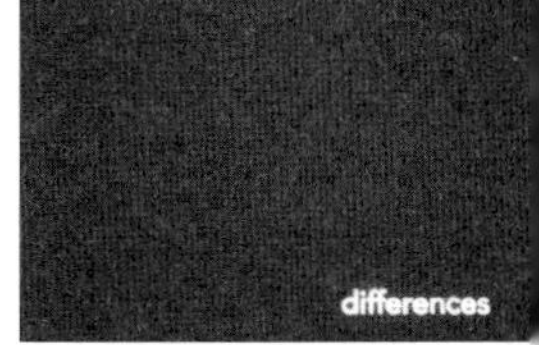

[Listening] Looking for answers, completely confused about sexual difference in the 1970s, I make an emergency call to several Italian feminist writers and thinkers of Ketty La Rocca's time.

'Don't forget that family and security is a facist slogan', the art critic and co-founder of Rivoluzione Femminile Carla Lonzi says. 'Equality is what is offered as legal rights to colonized people. And what is imposed on them as culture. Culture is the principle through which those with hegemonic power continue to control those without'.

'Take your own life, your own experience as a starting point'. The women of the Libreria delle Donne in Milano write. A politics that is based on equality, measures along the institutions and authorities that men have created to protect their own interests and privileges. 'Patriarchy was not only the control of men over women's sexuality. It was an entire culture: even a row of cultures with their institutions, religions and laws. That's why we put our relationships in the centre, something that would replace the marxist we and the liberal I.'

Gloria Anzaldúa, the Mexican writer of colour says, about the same 1970s, on the other side of the Atlantic: that it takes her tremendous energy and courage not to acquiesce, 'not to capitulate to a definition of feminism that still renders most of us invisible'. And that she will tell me later more about 'the unmentionable, never mind the outraged gasp of the censor and the audience'.

[Reading] She tells me to contact bell hooks who would say: 'As long as women consider freedom as the social equality with white men of the ruling class, they must have an interest in oppressing others as well.'

I think again of the Italian workers coming to Switzerland. The role they had back then is replaced by other migrants doing the care work and the reproductive labour so that the more privileged women can achieve equality with men.

I need to get back to now. In a last intention I send an e-mail to Philippe and Sophie. They tell me to accept that: 'The western gender hierarchy, as well as the critique of this hierarchy – the way it is articulated in western feminism – is part of the eurocentric modernity of the west. That this gender hierarchy itself was and is a central element of imperial power.'

On the way back:
Differenza becomes differences again
Desiderio desire

On the way back:
the train stops in Chiasso.
The border police enter.
Your passport please, they usually say.
A new border has replaced the geographical one:
The border police pick passengers out by their skin colours.
The train continues as a *white* train.

White is the name of the first class and *white* is the name of the second class of these trains that cross the border in Chiasso these days.
White is the name of the genders that cross the borders between Italy and Switzerland these days. I feel complicit every time in my invisibility with this new colour line, based on racial profiling, which means: me and you, the western universal I.

Reinforcing the I

Destabilizing the I

Eating the I

Unlearning the I

The I Today: I am a fiction

Reinforcing the I

Destabilizing the I

Eating the I

Unlearning the I.

I am a fiction.

[Playing *Flights of Fancy* by Maggie Payne]

[Credits]

Text references

– *Manifest ausländischer Frauen* (Manifesto of Foreign Women), Zurich 1975
– Ketty La Rocca, *Supplica per un'appendice*, Archive Books, Berlin 2010
– Giovanna Zapperi, *Spaces of Self. Femininity in Italian Video*, Centro Cultural Montehermoso, Vitoria-Gasteiz 2011
– Gloria Anzaldúa, *Speaking in Tongues. A Letter to 3rd World Women Writers*, in *This Bridge Called My Back. Writings by Radical Women of Color*, Persephone Press, London 1980
– bell hooks, *Black Women Shaping Feminist Theory*, in *Feminist Theory. From Margin to Center*, South End Press, Cambridge 2000
– Alice Walker, *What White Publishers Won't Publish*, in *I Love Myself When I Am Laughing… and Then Again When I Am Looking Mean and Impressive. A Zora Neale Hurston Reader*, Feminist Press, New York 1985
– Kathy Acker, *Against Ordinary Language. The Language of the Body*, 1992
– K. Hostettler, S. Vögele (eds.), *Diesseits der imperialen Geschlechterordnung. (Post-)koloniale Reflexionen über den Westen*, transcript, Bielefeld 2014
– M. Lonzi, A. Jaquinta, C. Lonzi (eds.), *La presenza dell'uomo nel femminismo*, Scritti di Rivolta Femminile, Milano 1978
– Carla Lonzi, *Sputiamo su Hegel. La donna clitoridea e la donna vaginale e altri scritti*, Scritti di Rivolta Femminile, Milano 1978

Sound references:

–*Estrogen* by Ravioli Me Away in 'The Inevitable Album', LP 2014

Reina is broadcasting from her bed. In bed she reads and she writes. There are books and pizza boxes, heaps of black clothes and a sleeping bag; involved are friends and people that call the radio studio, neighbours, caretakers, raindrops, listeners and death.

The performance is being recorded and replayed in a loop. A sign language translator accompanies the reading, also translating the sounds and movements of the performer. Both are in summer shorts and rain jackets. A red light bulb indicating that the broadcast is going on air.

[Recording a soundscape of clicks and overdubs, indicating the beginning of a noise concert. The recorded sound becomes the back ground of the following text]

Usually when interpreting

a score or a notation

people would wear black

black clothes would be

the symbol of the interpreter's neutrality

usually when we would listen

to complex texts or sounds

most people would close their eyes

a darkness that accommodates

[Dropping sounds]

[On air: red bulb on]

several calls reach the studio
people enter, they cry

it rains
constant drops
small waterfalls
a temporary liquid sound wall

Reina, you cry!
We are on air

we are in bed
we are in bed, on air

Reina, you cry so much!

A rain jacket
to cover from the drops
from the flood

the rain
the sound wall
a soundscape that isolates
interior from exterior
the world out there – around

[Digital delay]

out of convenience,
I say I
you say you: are here
I say I can

hear
I say you are we
she says she is them
you say he is:
they
the other parts
more than the other parts

all great revolutions
were planned in bed
Reina says

Reina reads
through the curtain of falling drops
voices that speak
her immobility
her isolation

listening
from her bed
to wet summer streets
as we do or do not pass –
Reina was convinced:

any body these days
can be turned into
a potential borderline

[Digital delay]

'don't let the fascist speak'
Pat Parker
on the other side
on the other side

of the water curtain

the rain, the flood, the tempest, she says
won't wash the racism in these streets,
in spoken- and unspokenness
of German cleanliness and efficiency – away

white privilege as it operates
a disease
Reina used to say,
that also sucks my life energy out.
Expanding, filling space and time
talking taking space and time
filling other people's minds
owned or:
ignored into inexistence

Reina reads
in bed, it rains

[Drops, louder]

the rain: an invisible acoustic curtain
between there and here
the sound of the interior space can be heard more easily now
even if: it's always there, all the same

Reina reads
through the curtain of falling drops
voices that speak
her immobility
her isolation

Reina dies
drops drill into the suspension of time

The broadcast is still on:

we receive a phone call
it's our neighbour
from an other place and time
across the street again!

Is she our only listener-
witness tonight?

She complains:

[Digital delay added to the voice]

Did you also think that this noise all day was a drill?
Speaking about revolutionary anti-fascism again.

how can any revolution not be cultural
how can anything not be cultural
how can any kind of politics not be cultural
how narrow is your understanding of what culture is

a drill?

Breaks through the water curtain
crypto-fascism
or the master's tools that cry
for strong languages, names

Reina reads
it rains

Reina dies in her bed
it rains
Reina, we are on air

Reina we are in bed, on air
your tiny, restless fists around my head

care as confrontation –
Reina used to say
behind her books
the air full of waves
of circulating voices
embodiment
her slowly disappearing

Reina is dead
I speak all to myself

I fall face forward into the dark
as I open the door –
the air is impregnated, sticky, heavy

the humidity of the incomprehensible

I don't see you, are you still there?
the translator keeps moving their hands
keeps translating the words into waves –
movements that cut the air

you probably sit in your room and you listen –
do you have a room of your own?
Do you share? With how many others?

Listening affectively
constant movement
in and through relationships

with others
with knowledges
with spaces
an embodied presence
lifetimes of unlearning

Reina counts the shrinking amount of squares
that her body claims
as a transition space, a passage, an access

reading Glissant's texts on relation
rather than writings on bio-politics

'listening,' she said,
'is not only a biological capacity
but an emotional relationship
between people that requires trust'

another friend
visited, cared
most of my feminist friends
she says, live alone

now that Reina is gone

a sea in between us
a lifetime keeps us apart
the darkness of histories unentangled
violated, swallowed, absorbed
incorporated, reproduced

the room has been inhabited
by someone else before
the word has been inhabited
by someone else before

let's break, let's pause
the production chain
Reina, said she had learned
how silence speaks: trust
an internalised awareness group
a proposition
from the protests
from the poets
handed over in daily conversations

don't lose Reina,
as the text unfolds
the texts that she reads
the voices that reach her room

I reach my hand out towards her
air, full of waves
bodies, full of memories
in this shielded room

a darkness that accommodates
a lightless surrounding
less observed
concentrate

listening, interpreting
combining the sounds of words
with smells, with hair, with looks
with gazes and desires
that allow us to see
our lifetimes connected
to rooms of resistance
as we keep listening

a last phone call reaches our bed, our studio
flooded, under water:

[Digital delay]

What is the interpreter wearing today? Something neutral, or something that makes noise, that makes the body and its movements: audible?

Along gendered colour lines
silent speech
protest
claims

planetary entanglement
intimacy, ex-timacy
embodied knowledge
esoteric, exoteric reading

unfinished sentences
a listening situation in which;
you can always step in, always call

[Someone is leaving a bath tube like Elsa von Freytag-Loringhoven would]

[Re-playing the recording in a loop]

Notes

Reina is the name of a friend who spent a long time in bed and in hospitals. Reina means queen in Spanish and is also a first name, 'llorar' is the Spanish verb for crying.

Text references

– Caitlin Cahill, *The Personal Is Political. Developing New Subjectivities Through Participatory Action Research*, in 'Gender, Place and Culture' vol. 14, n.3, 2007

Sound reference

– *Don't Let the Fascist Speak* by Pat Parker, in 'Where Would I Be Without You (The Poetry Of Pat Parker & Judy Grahn)', LP 1976

– *Standpoint, SHE* by Romy N., in 'Holding Tail With Mouth: Poems by The Baroness', Fytini, digital album 2016. fytini.bandcamp.com

'Since spring 2012, we have been writing and working on 'Jealousy Daily', a magazine that collects fictionalised accounts of jealousies, experienced and observed ones.' The text is a proposal for a contribution to the magazine and describes different ways of relating through intimacy and love – lived and imagined ones – all taking place in parallel. Involving words, and touch, and friendship, longing and loss.

The text was sticking out from behind a mattress for visitors to read during the exhibition *1x Medium bitte!*.

Above my desk, there's been a note for weeks, reading:

'Jealousy daily, I wouldn't have held back my emotions.
It's powerful, it's powerful'

It actually reads like this:

AKW:
'Jealousy daily, I wouldn't have held back
my emotions. It's powerful
it's powerful'

Your idea was to make some kind of a magazine for all the polyamorous among us, or for all those who have something to say about passions, secessions, obsessions. Like an A-Bulletin with B-messages. I wanted to write you back immediately.

We could write such a magazine via text messages.

Since your first message for our B-Bulletin, I changed my laptop, re-organised my flat, still didn't set up my studio, worked very, very many very different jobs and professions, conducted interviews, read books, wrote, took pictures, worked with students, thought about a possible PhD… And traded in my mobile phone and lost all my contacts – yes, these are excuses as well. And I've been incredibly busy with making sure that I wouldn't have any time to feel jealous. Now that I think about it, I realize that I've spent the last few months walking next to a certain person, feeding on my jealousy by staying so close, without writing any entries, ads or confessions for our B-Bulletin. At the same time, this also helped me avoid getting in close contact with other people I could have felt jealous of – jealous because of others again, of course.

Is there something like un-actualized polyamory? Or is it rather like with exhibitions, where only those count that have been realized in space, but not the ones that you thought out, in every detail, in your mind?

It's true that since our first entry for the B-Bulletin, we've rather talked about pendulums, commuting, wearing other peoples' shoes, and sleeping in allotment gardens – but maybe this is all connected. Maybe we're constantly producing messages that would have filled a whole magazine, but we didn't notice since we didn't write them down.

Your first entry, which has been pinned to the wall above my desk ever since (I copied it from my phone, since I traded in my old phone, as I mentioned already), has thus become something like an introduction, or an editorial, if we consider how voluminous our magazine would be if we counted everything that went by unrecorded.

Or maybe I should send you an audio message? A message to the medium or from the medium through the medium. In my job description, medium (in the plural and as an adjective) is about every third word, and I feel accordingly.

But we still wanted to do this bulletin, right? A bulletin, or a film, or a radio play – something made out of fragments.

Currently, I am interviewing a hundred people living in Zurich for a theatre play – that is, first I find them and then I interview them – maybe I should add another, unrelated question, since I also experiment with imagined characters (don't ask me how one can be bored in a job that eats away your days in an instant, but apparently it is possible) – and ask them how they feel about jealousy. But of course, I'm not really interested in this, it's only interesting to me if it concerns people I'm jealous of – and they normally don't want to talk about it. Except you! I'm glad there is this place, a meadow, where one can stretch out and say it loud and clear: HELLO! And we get all worked up in our jealousies and in the end, the world is full of people clinging to each other like glue, and we are glued to it as well and everyone wants to cling and be glued to even more and we are all lying on this meadow in a big pile, and we find ourselves buried at the bottom and we write our bulletin and we send our messages towards the top of the pile and everyone picks up one of the messages and reads it out loud and this results in a spoken concert, which we record and cut up and put together in new ways and yes, you can imagine what will become of it.

And I'm still concerned about the question of the water veins and why it's so difficult, if everything could be so simple. I was just reading that the dam of Lake Grimsel is about to be expanded and that this year, we (we: all of you with a car) were using our cars more than ever – right that year when we were so cautious after the nuclear disaster in Japan, it turns out we were using our cars more than ever, as a pure coincidence, and generally used up more energy than in all the years before. And the illiteracy rate is growing. And I guess we'll talk about women another time, once we've determined what this term actually means.

Or we could talk about the love letters we wrote but never sent. Of course, some will say now that this is completely obsolete and that they already did all of this with their novels, and that the novel as a form is obsolete as well and so is the text message novel and the TV soap opera – but here we come in and say NO!

You know what? Today I produced a radio show with five men for four hours and I really had to ask myself how the world got to be the way it is – and I also ask myself why I'm sending you such a long text now, you could even call it a letter, or a super long text message – when I could have done it all along? Still, I'm glad to be sending you something now, in my state of extreme tiredness with my eyes falling shut – but still typing with ten fingers.

You see, I am still trying to write my very own jealous messages and the bulletin will be a big hit for sure!

J'aime mes amies
Oui

Note

'A-Bulletin' is an alternative magazine whose hallmark are its many, often hand-written personal ads.

Digging into several directions, especially into the air. Catching waves and syllables. Taking around a life-sized image of Echo talking to Empathy and other figures that engage consecutively. Listening first and playing back later. Staged outdoors on a rooftop, the performance brings together recorded voices and uses a semi-mirroring foil, which, reacting to the light, covers or highlights who stands behing. A series of texts on glass accompany the performance.

WHO and HOW is/are – the they us invisible?

Who is invisible?
How is it to be invisible?
How are the invisible?
How are we?

'Time can fold and unfold.' Time she says, is gentle.

Time can fold and unfold she says. She says. She says it gently.

'Time is so generous, it is multiplying.'

Echo is not actually mute: Echo's way of speaking is the contrary of the tip-of-the-tongue phenomenon. It is the last bits of other's speech that she can throw back. Echo can speak through the words of others, can hear her voice in the words of others.

Considering speaking as an act of engagement, to articulate one's own opinion, expressing, one's own wishes in order to be heard: would mean that echo is mute. Athena took revenge on her by taking away her voice, leaving her with the last bits and pieces only. And also these as lingering sounds of what others have said – only if directed towards her.

Silent: the Mute-button.

Figuren die nur über eine
Eigenschaft verfügen.

Echo und Empathie im Gespräch:

Die Figuren greifen in die Handlung
ein, der Plot verselbstständigt sich.

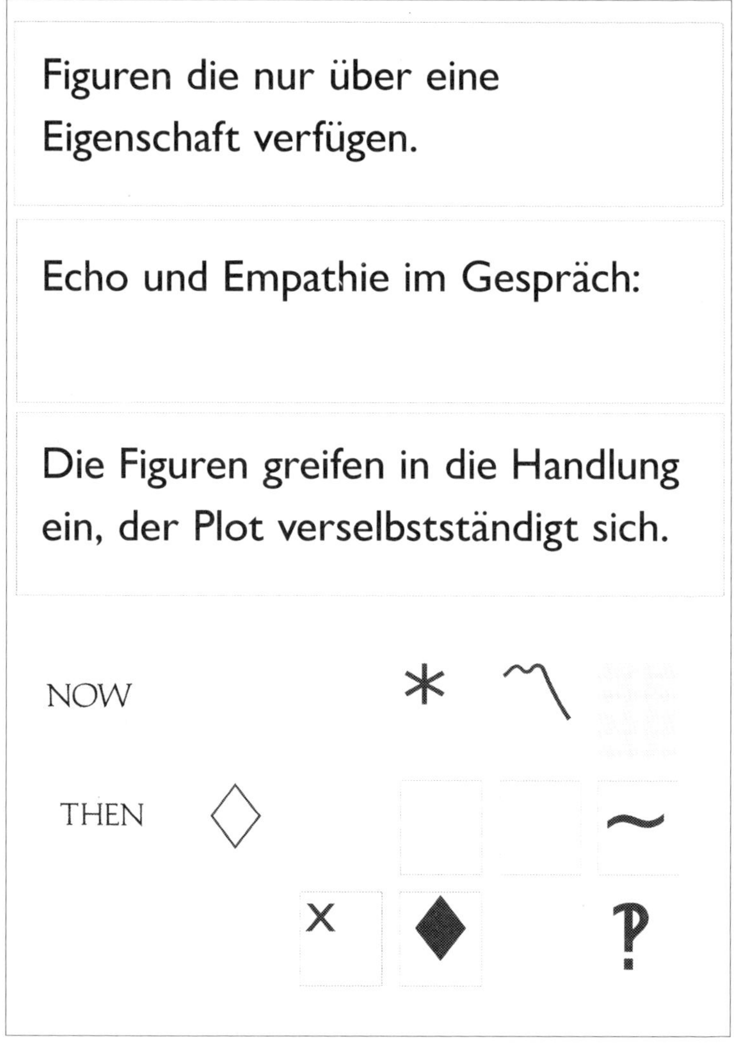

[Figures that only have one adjective. Echo and Empathy in conversation.
The figures intervene into the action, the plot becomes independent]

[Pressing mute on the mixer]

Mute is not the contrary of blacked out. Just because someone does not have a language, does not find their language anymore, we can not assume that there is not a linguistic body present.

Echo does not have a body, nor a clear silhouette. Not in the pictures.

In mythology Echo is characterized by her limited speech. And that the tone of her voice seems to be the one of a young woman.
No more is said about the appearance.

[Reading towards the mirroring foil]

Narcissus is not taking notice of Echo.

He as well acts through limitations. A figure that reflects itself in the opposite: the gaze fixed on itself, he does not find a way out of self-observation.

Echo stands, not far from Narcissus. She reflects the last bits of the sounds that encounter her across the waters. Narcissus does not understand her. The word pieces traverse above him; he is captivated by the attraction of his own image.

Echo as seen through a gendered active-passive dichotomy. The missing voice, without intended speech, the unexpressed longings, the unheard, and the wrongly addressed ones.

A body without a silhouette and a language that exists in resonation. Echo slips through the value systems that normatively define agency.

Archeology:

Is the activity of digging. Of removing soil. Removing soil and stones. To find more soil below that soil, older soil, meaningful soil.
What can be found can reach importance. The duration of digging is not in a direct relationship with how far back in times we dig.

Digging just in one direction, as if time was linear. A time that is imagined as a linearity – a succession of events that can construct a power similar in its potential as the assertion of bodies, the making of a self in accordance with another, the dropping out of the few from the many.

Digging into the soil. Opening up the soil. And how is it with the air. Digging into the air. Ablating the air, layer by layer. An archeology of the air, of the sky. And where do you lay the air, I mean the sky, I mean the layers, that you cross.

[Picking up the paper sky and folding it out, draping it over the railing, forming a background scenography]

A writing of history, along what we've been told:

In this other place you say, there is nothing to be dug for. That's why – in this other place – the digging follows the words, the directions of the words and the causalities that they might indicate.

Digging into several directions, touching lightly. Digging in the sense of: finding utopias, smaller or bigger enclaves of utopias, with all their colonial inclinations. Insisting. 'You seem convinced, that most of it lies in what can't be said or has not been articulated. And that all of it can be found in the skies.'

Along the strings of words. Digging clearly. Asking for the faded away and the not yet said.

Digging upwards, into the air, then into the cloud cover, the atmosphere and the homosphere, the troposphere and the stratosphere, layer by layer with small brushes and calm gestures.

[Ambiance whispers]

An archeology of speech and of reading, of listening and of listening towards, of handing over and of transmission. Radio waves and other

waves, entangled themselves with you. Waves that cross rooms, filled
up and emptied ones.

You are dragging these waves as invisible cords behind you. As you cross
the rooms, one hears murmurings and whispers. One thinks of the
texts that you have written, of the words that you were able to capture
momentarily, that you received back from Echo. When asked where
you had got all your words from, you said: very often I stand outside, on
the roof or at the river and I listen to the frequencies, how they glide
above the water, how they escape from the aerials, from transmitter to
receiver and also the other way around. Addressed and undressed notes,
mixed and recycled ones.

[Taking the picture of Echo from the railing, getting dressed in it]

Silhouette: that which stands out against the sky. Where the behind
engulfs the in-front-of and builds an outline.

Your body disappears, almost invisible. It is the silhouette that makes
the existence of a person, writes an Argentinian historian, referring
to the unclarified exigencies, referring to the death of the disappeared
ones. An attempt to find a material representation for disappearance.
For those who have disappeared, exactly for their thinking, and everything else that can not be defined by a silhouette.

The distinguishing features between body and mind, text and image,
measurements and disciplines.

[Stretching out the image of Echo]

In another, even more violent version of the myth it says: Echo had been
smashed into countless pieces. What was left of her, was only the voice
of a young woman. A young woman that is calling from afar.
A young woman that is calling from afar, that we can recognise in the

resonance of our own sentences, as they find their way back to us in parts. The unsent messages, the not sent wishes, the shortened sentences. The lost waves and censored frequencies. The plays written under other names. Ghost writings. Everything that is marked as anonymous, before anonymous of the digital age.

The body-less voices, frequencies that cross what otherwise depends on passports, income, origin.

Recognized as literature, the successful description of poverty, oppression, persecution and war receives honours sometimes. The media even make their income with it. But the people that belong to these stories are not wanted by everyone here, in reality, I realise as I see the results of the last vote on immigration. Suddenly it would be too full here, it is said, this terrace would be full and the rooms would be full, and the stores would be emptied and the rivers as well.

This is for sure not how it would be. However it would be, I would prefer packedness or emptiness to this declaration of self-entitlement to hate and to judge over the luck and life, sometimes even the survival of others.

[Playing *Love song for Alina*]

Words that cross the air, and in any second will collide towards, our, your and their inner ear.

You comfort yourself, that's normal – because you do not understand, because you do not want to understand, that it is not the same, if someone crosses the air alive or dead.

A block of words exceeds your mouth and crosses the air.

In whose words is it that we speak? In whose words is it that we speak.

I agree. In other words: I disagree. Still we write. Still we can write. In our words. Still we can describe the time we live in in our words. Write,

and call it for 'in our words'. Knowing where these words come from
and who is inscribed into them.

Assuming that writing always contains an echo.

Who has written me. Who has invented my story. Whose words am I
following, who wrote my plot. My body that along the words sticks
up into the sky, displaces air and particles. My body, in whose hair
the radio waves of last Saturday are still caught, my body, that grinds
caught data overflows and signals behind a murmuring and whispering.

[*Love song for Alina*, mute]

If I will fall he said, could you please stay?

My body got lighter I felt,
my life got less I felt,
parts of myself got lost in the sky,
because you got lost in the sky,
I felt

An Echo is what comes back to you and stays.

Time is gentle, she says. Time can: fold and unfold. We do have time,
she says.

'Also, archeology looks at discontinuities, transpositions and codes, and
not so much anymore at continuity and a translation of an authentic past.'

[Synthetic rumble]

Summer comes through the air, and doesn't come. The art events come,
and do not come. My friend comes over and doesn't come by. My girl-
friend comes, and doesn't stay. To come is to add something.

To undress, stripping off the silhouette, the ghost voices, the back pro-

jections, the words, material and immaterial words, the waves in the air,
the body in me and the body beside you.

As if time would correspond to places, as if time would fall into places –
this is how you were speaking about time, about 'Urgency and Emergency.'

[Synthetic rumble]

The conditions under which Echo and Empathy can raise their voices
are clear:

Echo can only speak when repeating after someone.
Empathy is in dialogue by empathizing with somebody.
Both are figures of interpretation and need to wait for others to say
something or to radiate somehow. They can only react to others. They
depend on others to express themself and to be noticed.
How can Echo and Empathy speak – to one another?

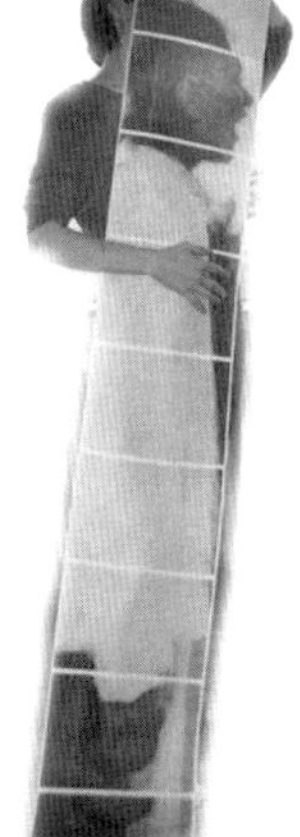

Sound reference

– *Scarcity* by Emma Hedditch, ICA London podcast, soundcloud 2012

Text reference

– *Journal d'Echo*, Les Complices* (ed.), edition fink, Zurich 2011

– Augusto Baol, *Theatre of the Oppressed*, Urizen Books 1979. 'The spectacle begins… The tragic
  herion appears. The public establishes a kind of empathy with her… The action starts… Suddenly,
  something happens that changes everything. A radical change in the carachters destiny.' 'Empathy
  makes us feel as if we ourselves are experiencing what is actually happening to others. Without
  acting, we feel that we are acting. We love and hate when the character loves and hates. Empathy is
  an emotional relationship between character and spectator'

This text notation of *5'5". 3 Renotations of 1 Act of Cleaning a Piano* introduces the private living and working environment in which the music piece by artist Franziska Koch was recorded: a shared house with a view on the lake and the Alps. The text takes the piece as a starting point to think about reproductive labour and maintenance work alongside value systems, discourses and movements that are gendered and racialized, claiming, in different ways, revaluation and wage.

A somewhat older instrument, inherited or from the thrift store. Maybe this piano has been given from a friend, or maybe you got it from your mother. It sounds like it has been tuned a few months ago and hasn't been played very often since. Bigger instruments like this piano tend to already be in someone's flat or life, somewhere next to you or behind you. They are similar to heavy stoves, built-in closets, hardwood floors, the refrigerator, the washing machine, and the tiles in the bathroom. I'm told this piano is being tuned regularly – if only half an octave too low. It is situated in a multi-person household and is often played by children.

Cleaning work in private homes should be remunerated, according to the leaflet Domestic work 2.06 of the Swiss social security administration, at the rate of CHF 18.20 to CHF 22.– per hour. The cleaning of the piano keyboard takes five minutes on the recording that is the basis for this notation. This would result in a total pay check of CHF 1.50.

You put the bowl of water on top of the piano. The top of the piano stays closed during cleaning. Here, the artist has positioned the recording device, to record the composition that results from cleaning and to document it for ensuing notations like this one. You move the chair in front to the middle of the keyboard. Dust has been gathering on the keys, no one closes the lid after playing. Through the skylight, mid-day light is illuminating the greasy surfaces. There is a window on either side of the piano. It's only now that you notice some gleaming fingerprints on the keyboard. Small fruit flies and minuscule flakes of skin have gathered between the keys. From the piano, you can hear the ticking of a kitchen clock. The instrument is situated in the dining room, separated from the kitchen only by a wooden closet. The distance between kitchen closet, mason jars, sandwich spreads, and the keyboard is only a few steps. That's why sometimes it's a little sticky – it's often played by children, I've been told.

A keyboard, according to Wikipedia, is an 'input device that is operated by pressing a number of keys with one's fingers.' The keys of piano keyboards used to be made out of ivory or ebony. For the sake of elephants and ebony trees, white and black coloured hard plastics nowadays imitate the original keyboard. Often used as well are laptop keys. The typed a corresponds to the played c, the s to the d, the d to the e. Laptop keys are normally made out of aluminium and synthetic materials. Depending on the surface condition and the products used, the act of cleaning produces some noise. Since I don't know if piano keys are cleaned with similar products as laptop keys, I do a search on the Internet: 'In either case, you could use a mild soda- or vinegar-based cleaner or an all-purpose cleaner. You soak a soft, lint-free cloth or sponge in it, then wring it out and use it to clean the keys carefully. After that, you can wipe them dry if you like.' Out of caution, ignorance and lack of experience, a regular cleaning cloth and a bowl of lukewarm water replaces the suggestion from the online forum for this interpretation.

The piano sits on a worn-out rug. But there is apparently no carpet in this room, next to the kitchen! The wooden floor is new but has no acoustic insulation, so it creaks whenever someone walks on it. The windows in the room that surrounds the piano are closed, and so is the door to the hallway. The small picture above the piano was painted by one of your kids and also shows a window. There is no chirping of birds around the piano, no honking of horns, no streetcar noises. There is no one else in the house, neither on this floor nor the next. You wear socks or you are barefoot, depending on the season. Your clothes aren't making any rustling noises and you neither have a cough nor a cold; your body silently follows the cleaning movements of your hand.

What kind of an interpreter are you? Is your work seen as play, as a job, as art? And is it paid accordingly? Are you cleaning your flat only for yourself, or are you cleaning for others as well? Do you have to rely on the cleaning? Are you receiving a pension that counts neither your domestic nor your artistic labour and you are cleaning to supplement it? Are you looking for work, or are you here for political reasons? Do you see your cleaning as an act of putting shimmering surfaces on paper, or of taking them off? Are you cleaning in black and white? Are you cleaning white surfaces on the black market? Are you cleaning illegally? (In the newspaper of the organisational committee for May 1, it says that there are 8000 undocumented domestic workers in the canton of Zurich, 90 percent of them women, precarious and without social benefits.) Or have you been hired through an agency and your job description on putzfrau-envermittlung.ch (cleaningwomenagency.ch) says, 'Your new cleaning woman [...] cleans your flat whenever and as often as you want [...] speaks and understands German [...] is our employee (we pay all required social benefits) [...] is always the same [...] can also do your laundry, ironing, shopping, watering of plants and much more (facility management) [...] We do your house work and you can enjoy your newly gained free time!'?

Even more likely, you are an artist and are neither paid for the cleaning nor for composing this piece. You probably see the cleaning of the piano keyboard as a way of producing a sequence of sounds and noises: a piece of music develops that results from an artistic method of composing that is based on the movements, gestures and tasks of housework.

Artistic and domestic labour: both activities are often paid minimally, sometimes more and sometimes less, and sometimes not at all. Not being paid well in the art world does not, however, mean that this work exists outside of the market, and especially not outside a neoliberal logic of valuation. What results from this overlapping of artistic and domestic labour is thus certainly not only the sound of a private and artistic space, but also of the history of you and of me in the history of everybody who came before, of those whose cleaning work has not resulted in a monument that could be filmed, no citation or photograph that could transform their history into one that could be verified and highlighted; instead there is the noise of scrubbing and grinding, sweeping and weaving, later the vacuum cleaning, and for a long time the opening and closing of the blinds, the scribbling of small numbers and messages on old newspapers.

Cleaning: domestic labour. Mostly still done by women, rarely remunerated with money. Cleaning as a method of composing music that plays with coincidence: if this work has been commissioned by a New Music Ensemble, it would be paid work. If this composition is created on your own terms – as an artwork within the so-called 'fine arts' – it might receive attention as a good idea, is maybe later rewarded with a work grant. To put it differently: if these two domains of mostly underpaid, unpaid or at least differently and often indirectly paid or rewarded labour overlap, there is not automatically a scandal resulting from this. Or at least not of the kind that is needed to bring attention to the extent to which women, migrant women, and women artists did and still do unpaid, underpaid or unrewarded work in many different domains; because the societal structures are organized in such a way, or because they are experimenting with different kinds of artistic work and artistic exchange than the ones envisioned by the canon of the respective funding instruments.

As it is written in the *Wörterbuch Soziale Arbeit und Geschlecht* (Dictionary of social work and gender), this kind of gendered work should be examined in regards to 'the conditions of economic exploitation and of socio-cultural recognition,' despite or precisely because of their historically rooted unprofitability. After just a few sentences and before producing any sounds, we have already come close to the bookshelf and the possibly both liberating and depressing blind spot of a post-Fordist society fixating on rewards and valuation through money, a society at the transition to the total economisation of one's entire lifework – a spot neither Marx nor Weber considered to be an important part of the capitalist system, a spot mostly occupied by women (in particular women from the working class, women of colour, and immigrant women), past and present. In an article from the online archive of the weekly newspaper 'WOZ', the feminist economist Mascha Madörin voices her frustration regarding the lack of discussion about paid and unpaid labour, and how important it is today to come back to the old feminist demands: 'There was a time when we wanted to reconsider and politicise both the working conditions in the factory and at home.'

Which institution and which time clock separates leisure and after hours from work in the case of domestic and artistic labour? 'On travaille toujours?' (Are we always working?) In their effort to overcome the bourgeois division between art and life, the Situationist International, for their part, promoted exactly the opposite – that is not to work – with their slogan 'Ne travaillez jamais!' (Never work!). This demand, however, is based on a conception of work, of art, and of art as work, which has been established by men during the time of industrialisation, and in which work is an activity that is over at the end of the work day. That is, a limitation of the work day for which the worker's movement, in tandem with demands for social benefits and better working conditions, had fought hard for. In contrast, and up until today, domestic labour – including care work and social work – has neither an end to the work day nor a system of representation based on recreational activities. Instead, never ending work days have always merged seamlessly into the next, without anyone creating a slogan for it. Some women's liberation movements (for example Wages for Housework) have therefore demanded, for decades, a wage for housework, not least to (retrospectively) improve the status of such tasks mostly undertaken by women. This demand has recently gained importance again, at a time when the current economic system is all too eagerly trying to incorporate any marginal, recreational, or subversive activity into its logic of economic exploitation – an act that often does not improve the recognition of the task at hand, but rather renders it more precarious – and at a time when it could be liberating (one would think) to be active in a domain that escapes this very logic. To be clear, we're talking about a capitalist logic of exploitation in which the 'Ne travaillez jamais!' has become the very motto of an increasing economisation of all aspects of our lives, a process that has brought it closer and closer to the 'On travaille toujours?' of housework. This has created a situation in which professional and artistic work, in their quality as work done from the home (office), and work days without beginning nor end are spilling out into our living rooms and coffee corners in a way that is similar to the workings of reproductive labour and the looms of the 18th and 19th Centuries.

To exchange 150 hours of factory work or housework for 150 hours of education: in educational programs created by labour unions and feminists in the 1970s in Italy, housework was considered equal to factory work. The Italian workers' and women's movements from back then, with their equal valorisation of housework and factory work, are still far ahead of our current understanding of these issues. Up until today, housework – similar to artistic labour – is not counted towards one's retirement pension and other social benefits, it is not tax deductible, and cannot be used in exchange for state-sponsored educational programs.

While you take the poster out of its folder and put it up on the wall above the piano, between the two windows, you're thinking about a sentence Paola Melchiori wrote in her article about the Free University of Women: 'Culture is a quality of life, not a quantity to be possessed.'

The demands of the women's movement to regulate and pay housework – to deliberately expand it to other areas, especially if questions of the private and the professional are getting mixed up with possibilities for subversion and strategies of refusal in new and unexpected ways.

Do you insist, when writing a proposal or application, on an artist fee? Something that has long been practiced in the world of theatre and music. To create less precarious conditions for us to stand, think, speak, question, discuss, translate and interpret for and with those recipients

and producers who cannot be reached by our voices if we do cleaning
work for others instead, or if we remain silent in an all too quiet way.
Another theme would be women, composition, and music making in the
home, but it's too late for this now as well,
the next boat is about to arrive in the harbour
and it will sound it's horn very loudly, and this is a noise that here
   and today we don't want to record or describe. The small keys are
sitting in front of you now, black on white.
  You position yourself in the middle of the piano and let your
 eyes wander over the keyboard, from the left to the right.
     You dip the cloth in the water,
        get comfortable on the piano stool,
        0'00" and start recording, playing.
                         You start cleaning
                    across the sounds   ʤ ɖ ħ ŋ
                       0'03" with one key (maybe an ä)
                       pretty far right on the keyboard
                   ⠿ and you're cleaning this one key
         f ɸʊ   with great attention,

              as if you were
          preparing for a virtuous play.
        A promising announcement of the musical play
       that now follows, by this first, now waning sound.
   0'07" Shortly thereafter you're ⱬ ʒⱬ

     sliding towards a minor chord, ⠿ ⠿ ⠿ which begins a little
   further to the left.
Your hand 0'11" ⠿ is moving ʜ ɟ ɬ ʁ regularly ⠿

     with slight pressure – a 0'12" movement   ⠿
     familiar   ⠿ from polishing shoes and which   ⠿
 is producing syncopes and melancholic sound sequences in our play.
           0'18" You ⠿ press two keys at once, quite strongly
               ⠿⠿⠿   then three and immediately again,
     whereby the first key slips away from the
     ⠿⠿⠿   ʤ ʊ   pressure of your finger.

β ç Following this is a chord
a little further to the left
0'29" and we're now in the vicinity ⚏⚏ of traces of jam
spread out ⚏ over some keys in the middle,
a child arm's length away from the stool.

It takes a little longer ʐ ʒ here
to move from key to key. ʤ ʐ ʒ
The scrubbing is persistent ⚏ ⚏
but careful not to rub
the jam ⚏ deeper into the gaps
between the ⚏ keys.

⚏ ⚏ **0'46"** You can hear
the piano hammers strike the stings,
ʊʒ ʃ ʒ when you press the keys down for cleaning.
⚏ ⚏ ⚏ A musical scale made of three notes,
briefly swiped over.
Again you clean the higher notes, this time ç H
with a little more pressure, creating
a small musical scale,
ending in a
combination of high notes,
⚏ ⚏ ⚏ ⚏ ⚏ ⚏
sounding atonal ⚏ ⚏ ⚏
θ ʊʒ ʤ
in their combination, ⚏
like cats ⚏ ⚏ ⚏
moving secretly over
There are, however, no cats in this house.
0'59" After ʐ ʒ
a double note ⚏ ⚏
and some highs ⚏ ⚏
⚏ you turn to

ʰʊ dedicate yourself patiently
and with medium force,
hopping from key to key
in regular intervals,
to the middle notes.
ç6 ʜ ䷀䷀
1'08" Now following are several
slowly pressed lengthy notes
䷀䷀

䷀䷀䷀ in the middle of the keyboard.
Mezzo forte ䷀䷀䷀䷀䷀䷀䷀䷀䷀䷀䷀䷀䷀ to forte,
you can hear the cleaning
f φʰʊ ䷀ ䷀ distinctively.
Several musical sequences and chords
䷀䷀   ䷀䷀䷀ pressed slowly
in the middle of the keyboard.
Mezzo forte ䷀䷀䷀䷀䷀ ䷀ ䷀ ䷀ ䷀ ䷀ ䷀ to forte,
䷀䷀䷀ moving slightly up
and down, ䷀ ䷀
1'34" ䷀䷀ ䷀ Already a little lower
1'36" in ䷀ ䷀ ䷀ atonal 3-note chords
and in ䷀ ䷀ ䷀
䷀ ䷀ ䷀ an excited mood
moving back ䷀ ䷀ ䷀ to the highs. **1'42"** ䷀ ䷀
䷀䷀ ䷀ ䷀ In the lower tones a descending
syncopated four-note chord in minor.
You ䷀䷀ turn your upper body to the left
and ䷀ again clean patiently in the lower notes,

ƀ θ ʊʒʃ

with the lower ䷀ notes almost falling into your hands,
and the cleaning producing a rumble.
䷀ A cloud obscures the sun.
䷀ ䷀ Very clearly, **2'17"**
䷀   a lasting, low note.

                  Followed by an indication
                      ☷ of ascending ☷ again,
☷ ☷☷ only to go back to cleaning on the far left once more,
                  around one of the keys.
2'35" Deliberately with pressure several times on the very low keys.
     You can hear how the floor is creaking under the weight of your
     right foot,
          which you press into the floor to stabilise your movements.
As if the sustain pedal was pressed, sounds reverberate from here over
               to the communal dining table
and to the couch, drowning out the ticking of the kitchen clock,
          drowning out the wood prints by Peter Emch on the wall and the
          magazines
     ☷☷ and newspapers
               scattered everywhere, ready to be read.
     ☷ An insistence **2'44"**
     ☷ on the second lowest note.
     ☷ *e* or *g*, earth's gravity. Maybe you are slightly tipping over
the left edge of the instrument.
               If we could see you,
we'd think of someone completely lost in her play,
or of a sound researcher,
     whose research increases the g-force
and sucks the fingers right into the keys.
☷☷ ☷ More low keys, medium loud.
     2'54" Now a melody
     ☷   tripping back ☷ and forth,
 like in a ☷ silent film
               when a thunderstorm is brewing.
Still in the lower keys. **3'00"**
     ☷   You are not sure if you play correctly?
If your reading and the translation of what you read
          correspond to the intended cleaning and pressing of
☷ ☷ the keys? If your interpretation is really an approximation
          ʦ θ ʊʒʃ   of the original, your reading an interpretation?

Low chords ䷜ ䷿ ䷦
  and single keys, ䷜
             cleaning intensively β çɕ ʜ
        ䷜ ䷿ ䷦ towards the middle.
           In the middle ䷁
        a little more ䷜䷜ extensively again,
        at the same time jittery,
      'almost baroque' as they might say on the
      crisis broadcast 'Diskothek im Zwei'
      (disco on channel 2).
    ䷿ ䷿ ䷦䷿   Firm strikes, several times.
  3'23"   Forte in the middle, ䷿䷦䷿ ䷜
and then back to the left side, ䷜ ䷜䷦
by pressing three keys at the same time,
      ䷜䷿䷜ several times, with deliberate strikes
back to earth's gravity,
䷜ *e* or *g.* **3'35"**
䷜ ䷿ ䷜ Soft taps, searching for the spots left untouched
    ʊʒ ʃ ʒ ʤ harder and deep,
䷜䷦   ䷜ like signs of coincidence or prophecy,
      whose name consists of a hint of what we wish for
䷜䷜䷜   and of what we think we see in them.
      3'41" As you shift some weight onto your feet,
        one can hear the creaking of the parquet floor.
        3'43" Without knowing
        ䷿ for sure if it's because of the kids,
       the cats, or the paint peeling from the ceiling,
     we are back again at this one key in the middle,
      we press it down   ䷜   ʒʒ   ʑ
     ䷿ again several times, bringing other keys down with it.
What does a sign stand for, and where does it stand ䷜ and with whom?
      3'49" How do we read, who tells us what we see?
        Some confusion in the higher notes,
          ䷿ ䷿䷿ ䷿ up to the highest ones. ䷀ ䷀䷀
            Your arms seem long enough.

Alternating
multi-note chords towards the
ꟼ꒧ ⰑꞀ Ƨ ⱬ   middle.
4'13" Several double notes, gently,
each pressed twice,
ascending, in the same tonality
until the highest note of the piano.
4'32" You strike the whole keyboard a few times, with great bravado,
from the lower notes   to the higher ones
and back again, β çᴇ with little pressure this time, so only a few
keys in the higher
and the lower tones are audible. 4'44" A jazzy rumbling in the
lower notes now, ascending and increasing towards the middle.
A high 4'51" single note,
a quick swipe across the whole keyboard, from the right edge of
the instrument to the left.
Again a few loose notes on the way back to the right.
Very quickly, as if you were in a great hurry, you lean against the piano.

You can hear how this creates pressure on the wood of the instrument,
right before your hand finds the stop bottom on the recording device. 5'05"

You get up, you open the window to the fresh air, the chirping of the
birds, the boots anchoring in the nearby harbour, before they head south.
You let your gaze wander across the Mediterranean Sea; since the 1980s it
wanders like that, every year, just as you drive across the keyboard, from
the left and from the right. The recording technique has since changed
considerably, and thus so has your play.

The next recording, in the coming spring, will sound differently yet
again, since you'll move and so does the piano. Anna, who's meeting you
for a coffee, will be at the door shortly.

It's ringing. The interpreter is on the telephone. Did you play correctly?
That is, play correctly according to this notation, which understands the
translation of audio sounds into written language and signs as an approx-

imation – in a language that invites you as the interpreter to bringing in your own way of reading.

You arrange the room around you the way it is described in this notation. The transcription of a sound recording into written language and signs on paper.

The notation describes, maps out, dictates and approaches you – you and your demands and wishes, the things you have to say, so you will play it. If you should play or read, and with which keyboard.

On a toujours
travaillé. idiots

Note

The house in which the piano is situated is a former squat – now a housing cooperative – at the foot of the Zurichberg, an area most known for its villas and expensive rents. The squat and the art scene around it was grounded in Zurich's youth movement, beginning 1980 with the Opernhauskrawall and claims for funding for non-established art spaces and practices.

Alongside sentences from Kathy Acker's essay *Writing, Identity, and Copyright in the Net Age* (1995), the performative writing builds up as a labyrinthine path through digital folders. Addressing an unknown finder, it is as much a play with forms of private writings, confessions and staging secrets as it is an interrogation of how the writer was separating friendship from what can be incorporated into the free market.

- In my confusion, I look to older writing.

- I look to find a clue about my own writing.

- As I continue to read, her words clarify more and more of what I, and perhaps many of you, are feeling right now.

- She is not talking about a master narrative.

- She is talking about language as it moves from one point to another point.

[Bannerfish.gif]

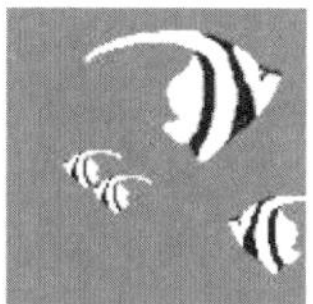

- She is talking about meaning as it reveals itself and so is co-equivalent to language.

- And perhaps this is how literature works.

- I do not write out of nothing, or from nothing.

- I must write with the help of other texts.

- Be these texts written ones, oral ones, those of memory, those of dreams.

> This is not background listening
>
> [Song for Aline.mp3]

- This is what we as writers do.

- Many of the people of this society are preferring to engage in writing.

- And in writing activities.

- Outside the realm of books.

- Once more we need to see what writing is.

- We need to remember friends.

- That we write deeply out of friendship.
- That we write to friends.

- We need to step away from all the business.
- We need to step to the personal.

- Our job is to hear and put together narrations.

- And so to give meaning even to what seems to be or is inhuman.

- The verb 'to own' must be questioned.

- I suspect that copyright as we now define it will become a thing of the past.

[Dear Finder.pt]

Dear Finder,

How does it feel

To carry a chain of data around your neck?
A materialised data cloud in which work – such as this – is waiting to be found, to be read. A secret, so far known to itself, the artist, the curator. To you the finder – one that shows or one that hides its treasures.

This is a slide show

A presentation – in which the words perform themselves. A flow of thoughts and visions, a gathering of words, images and music, a re-combination of existing sentences.

My work is data

It finds itself on sticks, on external hard disks. Where the scripts and images, the texts and instructions, the scores and dance steps pause for a while.

It will be a show

that doesn't show what you are reading right now. Packaging and jewelery, Post Internet Art, Post Studio Art, New Materialism, New Feminism.

Maybe

you are looking for something that makes you laugh and smile, that makes you feel beautiful and happy. A happy helper in a collapsing world.

The slide show starts, it rotates itself (you don't have to shift slides). It presents itself, it presents no self.

It rains

He sits on a couch in front of the windows. He reads. There is little light in the room. I start taking pictures of him as he sits and reads.

Finders Keepers

Do you know what you are looking for?

A Song

'Smoking is a pleasure. Smoking I wait for the one I love. It is an endless, pleasurable vice.' (Tita Merello)

In art there are no secrets
Openly.

You were looking for something elsc?
Try another data chain.

To let you know
another secret, another inside.

How to expose it
later.

A Presentation
A Beamer on the floor, between mattresses and cushions.
The sound should be placed between the mattresses, so it can be heard low.

The Internet
I've heard about it, my grandparents used to talk about it frequently.

Secrets to be told
Delete a white western male genius out of your canon every day. It will make you feel better.

Materialism
Is not a very interesting term when used as a token, we might agree.

[Read me.rtf]

the projector is directed towards the curtain
the projection can be seen from the back side of the curtain
a small wardrobe, open
a costume can be found inside the wardrobe
the curtain divides the room partly
open the presentation
choose 'full screen presentation'

- The literary industry depends upon copyright. But not literature.

- Business has become too heavy, too dominant.

■ We need to remember friends.

■ That we write deeply out of friendship.

■ To write is to write to another.

[Dear!.jpg]

Dear!

You guessed right: it was the last e-mail I received in the old year, and the first one I would read in the new year when returning to my mailbox. When you wrote it – if I am calculating the time-difference right – I was still celebrating.

Celebrating in a language that I do not fully understand. Being forced to listen closely and still never being fully part of the conversation, enjoying the liberty of interpretation that this gap of understanding opens up and following any train of thought as a sideline, drifting around in fantasies whilst sitting and eating in a chatty group, where nobody expects you to really participate in the conversation.

It makes me happy to read that you are spending these weeks in the South, enjoying lovely summer nights, seeing your friends and your family, having a break from studies. I would be curious to hear a bit more! Will you send me the paper that you are about to present?

Somehow there lies a little booklet on top of a bunch of publications on my table. I will present these publications in a few days, I was asked to connect them to something personal.

I took this little booklet that lies on top of this bunch of publications in an exhibition in Buenos Aires on Félix González-Torres' work, the same year as we spent new year's eve together. I didn't know his work, I didn't know much about art. I kept it and I sometimes come back to it. It is so simply made. There is this picture of Gertrude Stein's grave on its cover – I found out a few years later. It contains an excerpt out of Roland Barthes' *A Lover's Discourse*. Framed by the sentence, a modo de introducción – recently I discovered this sentence had been added by Alejandro Cesarco. It is funny that I kept this booklet and step by step I find out why it caught my attention.

An exhibition by Julie Ault, wherein I would find a booklet dedicated to Félix González-Torres' collection of clocks, and a performance by a friend who'd use excerpts out of an interview with Gregg Bordowitz comes to my mind whilst I am sitting and seeing the one-hour of daily winter sun passing over.

It is good to know that you have a health insurance that will cover the costly medicine so you don't have to tell your family if you don't want to, or to ask anybody else to pay it for you.

Where are the borders of society, how does a society construct itself by pointing out borders, by telling what is normal and what is not, what is a disease and what is not, what is a treatment and what is not, who belongs here and who does not.

What does it mean to know something about someone, what is personal about knowing and sharing, where does knowing and sharing get personal. [...]

■ Friendship is always a political act.

- Writing, narration, then, allows us to be human.

- That we write to friends.

- To write is to write to a stranger, to a friend.

Text reference

- Kathy Acker, *Identity and Copyright in the Net Age*, in *Bodies of Work*, Serpent's Tail, London 1997

I've been asked to write a response for this publication.[1] I'm writing from the perspective of having witnessed some of Romy's processes and performances, and having read these texts during their editing. What emerges is a response to a working method.

Romy writes,

'Words that move along – from one body to an other'

and later,

'In the archives I do not find anything about you, the witnesses are all dead'

I think Romy and I share a question.

How might we listen together to what cannot be heard, what is excluded, and cannot yet be expressed?

Recently, I've been thinking about reparative listening; reparative not in a sense of gendered, racialised and classed caring labour fixing a broken system, but reparative in a sense of... Is there a point at which, if enough people listened differently, the system might collapse and something reparative emerge? These thoughts bring together theories, queer, critical, anti-racist, feminist. I read and listen but often struggle to articulate myself clearly, to find the language right there on the skin of my fingers. A friend has been making paintings of eyes and mouths on hands, asking one to imagine what the eye would know if it touched, what the hands could know if they allowed some kind of entry. I think perhaps that Romy has auditory passages opening on the ends of her fingers, openings allowing entry. I think of her reading in archives, gathering, accumulat-

---

1   Romy and I have worked together before, once in Zürich for *Speaks with Silence*, organised by Romy with Side Room and OOR, and once at Transmission Gallery, Glasgow where Romy made *Reina llora*, Reads* for an event, *Undoing Listening*, that I organised in 2017. At this second encounter, there was sign language interpretation, and Romy responded to this by incorporating the figure of the interpreter directly into the text and staging of her performance.

ing, sifting, editing, assembling, reconstructing, stirring, taking things in to breathe them back out living; a circulation that is repeated when she asks the audience to move around as her body makes the space where they must listen to the carefully collected fragments of neglected and violently suppressed narratives. And the voice that speaks refuses to speak loudly, instead it insists, it demands… Come closer, listen more carefully, come so close that you have to touch and be affected.

*

A note to Romy and to you.

While we were reading we were writing. While we were listening we were writing.[2]

Editing is care work, editors are 'caseworkers for the commons'[3] editing the past into a common resource. Editing is additive, performative; speaking through. Being possessed. Having a mutable body that carries multivalently, simultaneously, in quantum spacetime. There is dirt on your fingers, on the skin of your words, as you sort through the archives. Artist. Editor. Feminised labour in many cases, including ours.

Collecting: additions, specifics, eliminated materials. Banding together.

*

'After all, totalitarian regimes do not impinge only upon concrete reality, but also upon this intangible reality of desire. It is an invisible, but no less relentless, violence.'[4]

---

2   While I was making watching you/Olive Michel and Fred Hystère perform *Touching Tones with Tender Buttons* in OOR Records, I was writing another text that is also this text. I wrote you an email afterwards. While I was projecting captions and watching you/Romy Rüegger perform *Reina llora*, Reads* with a sign language interpreter in Transmission Gallery, I was writing this text and another text that remains as yet unwritten. While I was reading your translations of the texts in this book and copy editing them, I was writing notes, some of which are in this text, along with notes that you wrote in return. There are quotes from your texts and from others here too.

3   Sarah Blackwood, *Editing as Carework. The Gendered Labor of Public Intellectuals*, 2014. avidly.lareviewofbooks.org

4   Suely Rolnik, *Deleuze, Schizoanalyst*, in 'e-flux journal', issue 23, 2011.

Careful seeking,
carefully seeking,
carefully, seekingly.

Writing a quiet voice thinking round the edges maybe, 'the little edges.'[5] Taking listening walks in your grounds, I 'walk as if the soles of my feet were made of ears.'[6]

Texts that were written to be spoken. This text was written as spoken, it was transcribed from your speech, indirectly. It notes the small refusals, it notes the large insertions, it notes the effort, it notes the care. The dirt on her fingers is accompanied by anger.
Her voice carries it steadily, forcefully. Listen. She imagines on towards an equality through her writerly care, through how she focuses her attention, because there isn't such an equality in discrimination.

She intends an interruption, another interruption, for she interrupts daily via her bodily non-reproduction, via her co-construction of networks of care, via her refusal and her excess. She is interrupting – 'Unlearning, undoing, undergoing, white privilege, hopefully confronting, transforming and shifting attention'[7]– in the loud, loud sounds of a contested now. A now that is everything that happened before and everything that might come.

(Turned inside or out, this *she* is plural. A *many*, a *they*, a *we*. A *she-not-I-her*, a *me*.)[8]

*

'First of all, trauma, in Greek, means wound, injury and it comes from the verb titrosko – to pierce. However… It was found that the root verb

---

5   Fred Moten, *The Little Edges*, Wesleyan University Press, Middletown 2015.

6   Misremembered line from Pauline Oliveros, *Sonic Meditations*, Smith Publications, Sharon 1971.

7   From an e-mail exchange between Katherine, Emma and Romy.

8   I'm responding here to a *she* that occurs in some of Romy's scripts, a *she* who is sometimes, often, the writer but who also slips and switches between bodies, temporalities and identities. See *Reina llora**, *Reads*, *Are You an Underground?*, *E lei qui sottolinea* and *Reading Recorded Voices*. This is not separate from histories of oracles, possession, ventriloquism and the everyday experiences of being a she.

is teiro "to rub" and, in this context, in ancient Greek it has two meanings: to rub in and to rub off, to rub away. Thus, according to the original definition, trauma is the mark left on a person as a result of something being rubbed onto him or her. Then, depending on the way that the rubbing took place there are two different outcomes. More specifically, when a powerful and intense experience is rubbed in or onto a person, the "trauma" could be either an injury (rubbed in) or a new life, where the person can start with a clean slate and with the previous priorities erased (rubbed off)'.[9]

I'm leaving these like this. Usually, it would be anybody, *but* any body *speaks better of the medicalisation situation. With border line there is also the option to make it borderline, which is used in the name* Borderline Personality Disorder (BPD). *I'm not sure if this is something that you're alluding to or not so I wanted to tell you this, that if you make it* borderline, *it also hardens the meaning of* border line *into something explicitly medical (and BPD is highly gendered, often a female diagnosis). I think you're referring to bodies and borders in the sense of migration and racism and no borders and so on, but there is this desolate hospital that we're in right now.*[10]

A world tangled up in words, bodies entangled in the material effects of violent discourses. This is where she points, where she inserts herself: amid the slippages, among the profusion of associations to take care of with each word written.'What opens up between two fields of language. A place in between. Between the inbetweens. Walking around in the inbetweens.'[11]

*

The subject object distinction is broken. It is constructed to break black bodies for its own existence and needs to be destroyed.[12] We're writing in English, the most violent existing language, trying to keep the distinc-

---

9   R. K. Papadopoulos (ed.), *Therapeutic Care for Refugees. No Place Like Home*, Karnac Books, London 2002.

10   Italics highlights in this text notes that I was writing whilst proofreading *If You Lived Here*

11   *If You Lived Here, You Would Already Be at Yours*, p. 16.

12   See Denise Ferreira da Silva, *Hacking the Subject. Black Feminism, Refusal and the Limits of Critique*, lecture at Barnard College in 2015.

tion fluid because it is broken. You do what you can with what you've got. How to write in English about the voice that these texts were spoken in, the movements that mapped them out in space amongst bodies. How to write in German about the voices that were never written down, to speak them into English, to say them out loud.

'In German "they" somehow would imply an implicit othering. In English this is not the case?' [13]

My spellcheck corrects othering to mothering and bothering. I am satisfied with both of these forms of action brought together now as an inseparable pair. I remember hearing Fred Moten talk about reclaiming mothering from capitalist social reproduction. Interrupting again. Existing antagonistically. Caring is affirming the space you want to be in that doesn't exist yet. But the word I intended to write is excluded from the normative structure of the computer dictionary.

It's because you started with someone. *In English you can use* they *as a gender neutral way of speaking about a person.* Someone *isn't the same as* one. *This is tricky because using one makes the voice sound detached from the situation, a different form of separation. I used* they, *it's more everyday so it puts the voice more in the situation. I'm not sure you can translate this concept of* one *very well where you can have a neutral subject that's part of the whole. Maybe in English* they *depends a lot on the tone of use in how othering it is.* But you're right, it's never mothering. *I often use a second person* you *to keep the subject/object distinction between the reader and the subject open but you can't do that here because of the previous paragraph...* [14]

---

13   From an e-mail exchange between Romy and Katherine.

14   Noted whilst proofreading *Are You an Underground? A Ship's Deck or a Terrace.*

'Without "separability", difference among human groups and between human and nonhuman entities, has very limited explanatory purchase and ethical significance.'[15]

You want to destroy the whole thing.

*

Because what Romy is getting at with her careful readings and assembled texts is the very thing that evades language: trauma. Sexual violence, racial violence, class war. The circumstances are everywhere and always, the mechanisms of oppressions are various, the power relations intersect and diverge. People harming people by action and omission. And pain, as Elaine Scarry says, is outside of representation, so it is difficult to share. In amongst the trauma, between the rubble and the dust, Romy is listening for excess and possibilities for thinking differently, insisting that we join her.

*

---

15   Denise Ferreira da Silva, *On Difference Without Separability*, in J. Volz and J. Rebouças (eds.), *32nd Bienal de São Paulo. Incerteza Viva*, Fundação Bienal de São Paulo, 2016.

A Response by Emma Haugh
In-between the performance of bodies

In the script *In My Confusion I Look to Older Writings* Romy refers to Kathy Acker who writes 'We need to step to the personal. [...] We need to remember friends, that we write deeply out of friendship, that we write to friends.'

We write to some known and unknown friends, not to a grand political ideal, we write with our bodies, conversations, gestures, touch, and the language is always affective as it is shared in time and space.

Here I write in friendship with Romy's scripts; as a reading of her work between and across the lines, allying hers with other writers' lines of thought.

I was interested in thinking about affect in relation to the scripts held in this book. What does it mean to be affected by a texts performative potential? What kinds of politics can the affects of performance in/as text make present?

Sara Ahmed

'How do emotions work to align some subjects with some others and against other others? How do emotions move between bodies?'

As I read the scripts included in this publication I went looking for the source of an anecdotal reference. A friend had told me that the Dj/producer/trans activist Terre Thaemlitz was critical of the work of the artist Wu Tsang, in relation to politics and affect. Thaemlitz critiques tropes of authenticity and innate attributes, institutional power structures, and the language of aspiration and positivity that 'enacts a reciprocal prohibition on negativity.' I think of Thaemlitz as a 'feminist killjoy' in queer space who disrupts the idea that representation is a desire of the marginal. I was curious as to what disagreement Thaemlitz might find with the queerly affective work of Wu Tsang. My friend couldn't locate the source for this piece of dislocated memory. Now, as I consider his misplaced or misunderstood reference Kathy Acker whispers over my shoulder:

'Citation and mutation
Mutate and resituate'

This failed searching for origin opens up folders within folders, links within links, anecdotes and quotes, much like the data chain that makes up the script *In My Confusion I Look to Older Writings*. I spend several hours following Thaemlitz's trail online.

Here Thaemlitz is sitting close to the philosopher/queer activist Paul B. Preciado upon a raised yellow platform, encircled by an audience bathed in shadow. A little awkwardly they share a microphone, sometimes holding it for the other, taking turns to speak. In-between their discourse and disagreement there is acknowledgement through gesture and touch. They seem to have known and appreciated each other via the others work. There is affection, perhaps for some time from a distance, now in close physical relation. This unfolds intimately, publicly, tangible across digital time and space.

Thaemlitz has her hand on Preciado's shoulder, smiles and says: 'I'm so intimidated by you, you're…'

The shadowy audience bursts into collective laughter. Thaemlitz laughs a laugh that leaves a smile on his face.

Preciado protests: 'No, no, I love you, I'm so intimidated by you.'

Thaemlitz retorts: 'Hey…no…too late. Every time I see you and hear you it really has such a big impact on me.'

Preciado says: 'I think you will be my male side or female side of my male side or whatever.'

Thaemlitz gazes at Preciado and says in a tone of momentary smiling submission: 'Ok.'

The exchange is flirtatious as they talk, touch and maintain eye contact for much of the conversation. Flirting as solidarity.

'Heavy Metal and all forms of love that do not exist in sex education classes in school.'[1]

1   *Language Is Skin – Points of Access, Points of Entrance*, p. 138.

They disagree on many points, 'I feel the same way,' Preciado says.

'I agree. In other words: I disagree.' [2]

'Friendship is always a political act.' [3]

Living, vibrating, somatic, voice

I have not seen Romy perform the scripts held together in this book, I have not experienced Barbara Hammer's films in full, I will never see the performances of Ian White. I know that the writing of Frankie Hucklenbroich is for decades out of print and that their friend, the writer/editor Lillian Faderman continues to give me permission to republish Frankie's difficult, tough and tender book *A Crystal Diary* that tells of Frankie's working class, hustling, roaming, street butch life in 1950s America. I will never speak with Frankie, except through their writing.

Invoking absence can be, as in the script *Who and How Is the Invisible*:

'An attempt to find a material representation for disappearance' [4] – or – 'A body without a silhouette and a language that exists in resonation.' [5]

---

2   *Who and How Is the Invisible*, p. 180.

3   *In My Confusion I Look to Older Writings*, p. 205.

4   *Who and How Is the Invisible*, p. 179.

5   Ibid., p. 177.

Hilton Als

'If you write it down someone will find it.'

But what will they do with it?

'The unsent messages, the not sent wishes, the shortened sentences. The lost waves and censored frequencies. The plays written under other names. Ghost writings. Everything that is marked as anonymous.'[6]

I had not seen the films of David Wojnarowicz until last night.

A Fire in My Belly is work I've read descriptions of, seen film stills from, held an imaginary for. I knew about David's lips sewn closed with needle and red thread, bubbles of blood around the piercings, I knew that he made space for his own agency, like Ian White. I knew that he made abundantly, a profusion of loose ends. I knew that he was angry and that he found ways to make his angers generous, available, and public.

What I didn't know, and what the curator Natasha Ginwala told the audience in Savvy Contemporary, is that *A Fire in My Belly* was part of a performance, and not made as a singular work.

David's, boldly symbolic, abject embracing, erotic, unfinished, films are silent. His living, vibrating,

6   Ibid., p. 180.

somatic, voice is not present, but it resonates in his absence, in the unexpected ways he might have followed one thought with another, in the omission of emotive expression carried from a voice into a room that sat absorbed in the echoed silence of David Wojnarowicz's untimely death, his unfinished-ness, the incomplete work of grief.

David Wojnarowizc   'It becomes too much after a while. Seeing so much death, hearing of so much death, feeling so much loss. I wondered recently if I was becoming numb to the idea of death itself. What was in the mid-1980s a recognition of loss so profound upon hearing of the first person I knew who had just died of AIDS, had slowly become so familiar that I wince upon hearing that someone new has died and then tuck it somewhere in my psyche and try to refocus my thoughts to something simple like paying the rent or buying the food for my evening meal.'

In the absence of David's, living, speaking, body, there remains:

Fred Moten   'A spooky resonance, a phantom hapticality.'

Propped up at the counter in the cafe K-Fetisch in Berlin Romy and I talked about archives, what is kept, what is taken care of, who believes their archives worth maintaining, what gets lost.

Barbara Hammer   'One thing is how things get saved and who gets attracted to it, and that's true not just for lesbians, it's true for women, it's true for blacks, it's true for Latino's and Latina's.'

As we consider what gets lost our conversation dissolves into a quiet pause, there are no words for this, only the possibility of being attentive to those lost pieces that we do find.

'Listening, she said,
is not only a biological capacity,
but an emotional relationship
between people that requires trust.' [7]

It's not about essence it's about alchemy

In another recent conversation, the writer Amelia Groom said: 'It's not about essence it's about alchemy.' We were talking about performance, identity, writing and experience. Amelia's comment is helpful for those of us who are considering how we might approach acts of 'writing ourselves in' or acts of writing others in, when institutional desires tend to focus on and fix perceived essences of otherness.

Octavia Butler

Fred Moten

'Deviance is not opposed to the norm, it comes before it.'

Terre Thaemlitz

'The reality that most forms of transgenderism and gender deviance rely heavily on disobedience and non-cooperation.'

When essence as otherness becomes artistic currency then a reflexive trickster performance is

---

7 A reference to Caitlin Cahill's *The Personal Is Political. Developing New Subjectivities Through Participatory Action Research*, in *Reina llora* Reads*, p. 165.

necessary to deliver but via a non-performance (or drag performance) of any prescribed essence. The transmutation of matter, experience, positioning and flesh allows one to say what needs to be said without pinning the heart, skin, face or genitals to the walls, performance platforms or publishing apparatuses of institutions for public inspection and appraisal (unless one has the desire to do so, which is sometimes the case).

Fred Moten

'Is there a way to subject this unavoidable model of subjection to a radical breakdown?'

Terre Thaemlitz

'Being put into the game only multiplied my troubles.'

Working essence as alchemy reminds us of the necessity for filters, layers and transformative processes when it comes to the making and publicising of work that deals with personal biography, 'anti-normative desires', stories and visual languages that speak from 'outside of the outside.'

Fred Moten

Jose Esteban Muñoz

'Because the archives of queerness are makeshift and randomly organised, due to the restraints historically shackled upon minoritarian cultural workers, the (political) right is able to question the evidentiary authority of queer enquiry.'

'Instead of being clearly available as visible evidence, queerness has instead existed as innuendo, gossip, fleeting moments, and performances that are meant to be interacted with by those within its epistemological sphere-while evaporating at the touch of those who would eliminate queer possibility.'

Institutions don't need to know that alchemical processes are active within the work, the signs will be read and understood by dispersed and tentative communities of friends and strangers who recognise one another's expressive languages across shared experiences.

Talking with Romy about essence we came to a consideration of essence and smell, how smell interrelates people, rooms and objects. How smells change, depending on the seasons, rays of light, heat and air pressure, and how this opens out the potential for essence to be non-identitarian and queer, blurring the distinction between humans, objects and their surroundings.

It might be possible to leave a trace of one's smell, a lingering, ungraspable essence, an unavoidable intimacy, behind us in the institutions as we move through them on our flight back to the margins, those places where we know that we are many, not singular.

'listening affectively
constant movement
in and through relationships
with others
with knowledges
with spaces
an embodied presence
lifetimes of unlearning'[8]

8   *Reina llora*, *Reads*, pp. 164-165.

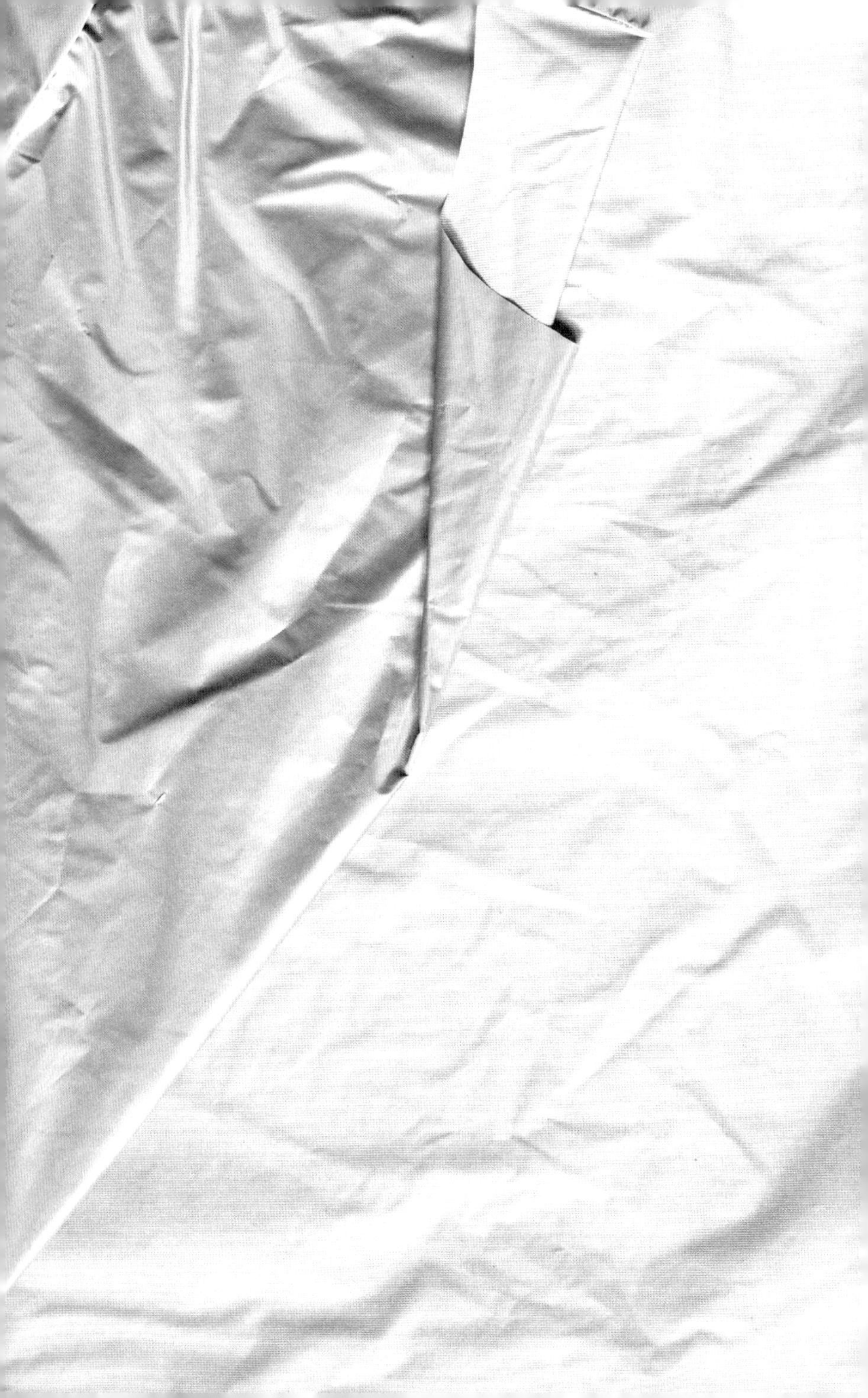

If You lived Here, You Would Already Be at Yours is a performance and an exhibition contribution at the former Material Testing Institute of Escher Wyss in Zurich within the 2015 exhibition *How to Play*. It was written in German and performed in an adapted version as part of the performance evening *Alice Toklas Reads her Famous Hashish Fudge Recipe* at Kunstraum Niederösterreich in Vienna and at Stadtgalerie Bern in 2015. Thanks to Gioia dal Molin, Sissi Makovec, Maria-Cecilia Quadri and to Baugenossenschaft Berufstätiger Frauen Zürich for generous insights into the archive.

Walk Along an Invisible Line is an audio play for a walk and a performance that was part of *A Word for a Play* by Franziska Glozer and Sarah Bernauer during Regionale, Basel, Freiburg, Alsace in 2012. French translation by Alain Volpe.

Climbing Monuments was voiced in Italian by Daniela Bertini, Lila Lisi and Anna Schlossbauer and performed in 2016 together with Flora Vannini at Museo Vincenzo Vela in Ligornetto on the occasion of an exhibition by Pascal Schwaighofer. English translation by Katja Schwaller and Spencer Rangitsch.

Sounds Like Metal was performed in a first version during the festival *The Other The Self* at Q-O2 Brussels in 2016. The version *I Am the Wall – Where Will You Be Main Frequencies* included here was performed during KAAI theater's *Performatik Festival* in Brussels and for *Soundings* at KHM Cologne, both in 2017. The script has been included as a visual contribution in *Grounds for Possible Music*, Errant Bodies Press, Berlin 2018. Thanks to the Q-O2 team and Franziska Windisch.

What She Said Before Leaving Society was read and performed at Lost Property in Amsterdam in 2014. Thanks to Maria Guggenbichler and Felicia von Zweigbergk.

All the Ways Are Open – Review of the Weeks is a performance and an audio work presented within Sinopale, Bienniale 5 in Sinop, Turkey in 2014, and in the 2015 exhibition *Collecting the Future* at Corner College, Zurich. It was performed in Turkish at Hal Binası Sinop by Aslı Ozan and broadcasted by Barış fm. The English script was included in part in the Sinopale Newspaper (2015). Thanks to Tayad Committe Schweiz, Berivan Güngör, Dimitrina Sevova. English translation by Alain Kessi and Frank Hagen.

A Fabric in Turkey Red – Reading Recorded Voices was performed in German at Kunsthof Zürich as part *of Opportunities for Outdoor Plays? Playgrounds – New Spaces of Liberty (The Question of Form)* and in English at *IPA Istanbul Platform for Young Performance Artists* in 2013. The version printed in this book was adapted for the book launch event *Publikation/Performance/live* of the publication *A Play for Recorded Voices* at Les Complices* in Zurich in 2013. Thank you Dimitrina Sevova, Andrea Thal, Georg Ruthishauser, edition fink and Les Complices*.

Are You an Underground? A Ship's Deck or a Terrace was performed in a longer version in German at Terrassensaal Kunstmuseum Luzern in 2015. A second version of the script is included in the publication *The Air Will Not Deny You*, Diaphanes, Berlin 2016. Thank you Andrea Saemann, Franziska Koch, Bernadett Settele.

Language Is Skin – Points of Access Points of Entrance was performed in German as *LOA* for the closing event of Souterrain and as *Language is Skin – I Like the Tone of This Place* the following day for the opening event of OOR, Zurich in 2014. It was shown in English and Greek as a choreographed space in the exhibition *The Other Design* at Beton7, Athens in 2015. Thank you Caro Cerbaro, Anna Frei, Elke Bippus, Sarina Scheidegger, Sofia Bempeza.

E lei qui sottolinea – Binary Codes as NO was performed in Rome in the exhibition *The Ketty La Rocca Reading Room* by Sally Schonfeldt and as part of Maria Guggenbichler's *Melancholic Afternoons* in the exhibition *Memory Machine* at Castrum Peregrini, Amsterdam in 2016. Thank you Anna Frei, Maria Guggenbichler, Radna Rumping.

Reina llora*, Reads was performed during Katherine MacBride's *Undoing Listening – A Publication as Doing Things Together in Public* at Transmission Gallery, Glasgow in 2017.

Jealousy Daily is a magazine initiated by Anne Käthi Wehrli and Romy Rüegger and was a contribution to the 2012 exhibition *1x Medium bitte!* by Anne Käthi Wehrli at Les Complices*, Zurich and to *Sex Matters* at WUK, Vienna in 2014. English translation by Katja Schwaller and Spencer Rangitsch.

Who and How Is the Invisible was performed as part of *Rooftop Readings* at LISTE in Basel and as a choreographed space and a visual publication contribution in *If Anyone Answers Scream!* at Oslo10 in Basel, 2013. Thank you Sarina Scheidegger, Chantal Küng, Franziska Glozer.

Notes for the Interpreter – On a toujours travaillé is a text notation, consisting of 14 cards and one poster, written for *5'5". 3 Renotations of 1 Act of Cleaning a Piano* by Franziska Koch, edition fink, Zurich 2013. It was partly reprinted in *Bodies of Work*, ed. FAK, Karlsruhe 2015. Thank you Franziska Koch, Anna Frei, Georg Rutishauser, edition fink, Lotte Meret Effinger. English translation by Katja Schwaller and Spencer Rangitsch.

In My Confusion I Look to Older Writings is a contribution to one of the USB necklaces of the exhibition *Use 2 be USB* by Rebecca Stephany at Rongwrong, Amsterdam in 2014.

Graphic Design: Archive Appendix

Copyediting: Paolo Caffoni

Translation of *Climbing Monuments*, *Jealousy Daily*, *Notes for the Interpreter*: Katja Schwaller, Spencer Rangitsch

Proofreading: Katherine MacBride, Cassandra Edlefsen Lasch

Published by Archive Books in collaboration with Scriptings/Berlin

Thank you for your support and your contribution
Achim Lengerer, Paolo Caffoni, Anne Retsch, Chiara Figone,
Katherine MacBride, Emma Haugh, Katja Schwaller,
Spencer Rangitsch, Simone Koller, Daisy Nutting

This publication was made possible with the support of Pro Helvetia, the Swiss Arts Council; Stadt Zürich Kultur; Stifung für Erforschung der Frauenarbeit.

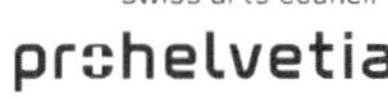
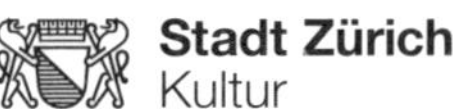

Archive Books

Müllerstraße 133

13349 Berlin

info@archivebooks.org

www.archivebooks.org

Printed by BUD, Potsdam 2018

ISBN 978-3-943620-76-4